THE ACCELERATED SOUL

THE ACCELERATED SOUL

What You Can Learn From A Spiritual Master

Walter C. Hurd

ISBN-13: 9781539051695
ISBN-10: 1539051692

Contents

Introduction

I once worked full time as a chef at the Hungry Mouth restaurant, a health-food restaurant owned by Walt Baptiste, who was one of those rare individuals who is born a fully realized spiritual master. I worked for the guru for fifteen years, but this is not a book about what it's like to work for a spiritual master. It's not even a book about Walt Baptiste—although both subjects would make great books. Instead, this book has two other purposes. It describes what happened to me and my life and how I was transformed once I immersed myself in Walt Baptiste's teachings, and it also outlines my conscious observations of the forces that cause internal transformation in us all when we choose to take seriously the efforts required for soul fulfillment and spiritual growth.

Writing a book of this type brings with it the joy of knowing that it will be a great help to people at some point along their life journeys. Many people enjoy the aha moments of new insight. They may believe that spiritual growth is akin to feeling supremely good after a Reiki session, a Qigong class, a really great yoga class, or perhaps even an inspiring lecture. These moments allow for a letting go that allows in a freshly balanced, aligned state of being—but they are temporary. What about the rest of life: the times between those aha moments and supremely good emotions? In my experience, every day sets the stage for some phase of spiritual growth.

Walt Baptiste taught us how to walk the Path of the Masters, the wondrous, invisible path that, if you are paying attention, lets you discover that every day is a step forward toward a life of purposeful, true meaning, spiritual realization, and *freedom*! I wrote this book to pass along to you the knowledge of the ever-present cycling energies of life, accentuated by the structure of Walt Baptiste's teachings. Its structure aligns the student with a steady, uplifting flow of consciousness expansion. Once people recognize the uplifting movement of their lives, their souls' evolution accelerates, and they find their inner alignment with the potential for spiritual experiences irresistibly compelling.

A few months after the start of my adventure at the Hungry Mouth, I was putting together the ingredients for a health shake when I was overcome with a feeling of joy and gratitude for the gift of being blessed enough to work so closely with a genuine spiritual master. Just then, Walt Baptiste entered the kitchen. I started bubbling over with a speech about what a great gift it was to work for him and how I couldn't be thankful enough for the opportunity. I also thanked him for building a place where I and the other students could "burn away" layer upon layer of old karma while benefiting from spiritual growth. During my babbling, I made a deeply felt vow to give my all to him and his work and to learn everything I could possibly learn from him. He listened calmly and then said, "Yeah, it's always a good idea to take one lifetime to focus only on spiritual growth," and walked out the back door.

Walt's simple, direct response came to me as a shock. I was twenty-five years old! I couldn't imagine a lifetime of intense experiences like I'd had in the first few months at the Hungry Mouth: they included working ninety five to one hundred and ten hours per week! Still, the idea of a lifetime of spiritual practice meant for discovering my soul and for spiritual growth stayed with me, and I began to realize just how important it was. Also, there was the compelling thought of who I might become and what my life would be like if I did continue for the rest of my life.

Somewhere inside of me, I committed. My commitment must have been on a deep, subconscious level, because for the next forty-plus years, with each major turn of my life, no matter how challenging or positive, I refused to stop using the soul-discovery and spiritual-growth principles that Walt Baptiste instilled in me. The truth is, I couldn't have stopped if I wanted to.

My reason for sharing who I have become and exactly how I resolved mountainous obstacles along the way is to demonstrate that success is possible for anyone with a passion to accept his or her individual adventure. I also wrote this book to demonstrate how adopting Walt Baptiste's teachings will enliven and refine anyone's ability to sense the finer faculties needed to build a relationship with his or her soul's reason for being. It demonstrates how these teachings refine one's senses to the level of realizing Spirit's presence within oneself and one's life.

Take a moment to think about this: during the last century, 1900 to 1999, civilized humankind has mastered materiality. The development of the sciences; ground, sea and air and even space transportation; systems of communication, banking, and commerce; the design and construction of heretofore unimaginable structures; and technological innovation that allows for social discourse on a grand scale have, to a large degree, been mastered. And all of this mastery will continue to expand throughout the coming century. But there is one area of human pursuit that is missing for the common person. It is the conscious recognition of the value of living the deeper reason for life *daily* and discovering the "reason behind the reason" for life—which is to expand one's consciousness to embrace the soul's mission for this incarnation and to cultivate a passion for the firsthand experience of the spiritual nature of the individual Self and of Life itself. Those who do these things will ultimately experience what it means to *live as a whole human.*

There is an interesting timing with this book. I think we can all agree that the world is in a cycle of very fast change. The trend toward mediocrity is giving way more and more to people's souls urging them to find a deeper meaning and purpose for their existence. Many cite a burning desire to be "authentic." These same people may enjoy material wealth and loving relationships, yet inside, they sense that something is still missing. When they take a moment to be honest with themselves, they find that they are deeply unhappy. The problem is that they never learned their soul's desires for this life or how to fulfill its needs, so a very important part of them still suffers. I know about these people. Many times, our work together started with a confession like, "I need help. I've lost my joy in life." So, for the past twelve years, I've worked privately with them, showing them exactly how to reclaim their joy.

Today, an increasing number of people enjoy many of the experiences I describe in this book, but they don't really understand why they are having them. These people, consciously or unconsciously, yearn for someone to look to—someone who has walked the same path they're experiencing; someone who, through personal experience, has already solved many of the riddles that are part of the "invisible path." And they yearn for someone who knows how they can overcome the obstacles they face.

Even more important, these people have no clear vision, no real knowledge of the beautiful, ever-new life experiences toward which they are being led. It breaks my heart to know what that vision is as I talk with them, and yet I cannot, under the circumstances, communicate it to them in our brief conversations. This book is for these passionate, spiritually astute individuals, and I look forward to delivering that larger vision to them.

This book consists of two Parts:

Part I tells the story of what happened inside myself and to my life over the past forty years. The story is integrated with the principles that Walt Baptiste taught and how they transformed me and continue to draw me toward the full expression of my Higher Self.

Part II takes a deeper look at the four main pillars of Walt Baptiste's teachings. It continues to draw upon the stories of how I learned by experience, but it goes deeper into the details and importance of each principle. You will learn how the four disciplines combine to create a steady flow of synergistic energies that heals one's past while setting the stage for uncovering the soul and the potential for spiritual experience.

Part II also describes what's needed to accelerate the soul's evolution while enjoying simultaneous spiritual growth. You can use its writing exercises to reestablish your relationship values and also to address directly the irritations in your current life situations and how to reverse them. Buried in these exercises is the opportunity to address your soul's needs.

In chapter 4, I describe the reliable cycles in life that affect your psychological evolution and, in turn, your soul's evolution. Chapter 5 defines the different sections of your minds: their nature and their characteristics. Each section has its own function and purpose and creates unique, separate inner responses to outside life. You will need this information to understand the inner purification process.

Chapter 6 offers examples, tips, and guidelines for processing the negative conditioning and emotional wounds of your past, and chapter 7 describes exactly how life can sometimes be very direct and personal in its communications with you. An undeniable direct and personal communication results in a new, deeper layer of understanding and inspiration concerning your Self and why you are engaged in your particular life's path.

Chapter 8 delves more deeply into each of the four disciplines: yoga; meditation; serious, health-building exercise; and a diet of healthful eating supplemented with vitamins and minerals.

Just before leaving my chef's position at Walt Baptiste's health-food restaurant, I worked for months attempting to become a perfect conduit for spirit to move through me and into the food I was creating. The result was a whole new experience and dimension of creating food. One morning, Walt Baptiste came into the kitchen to confirm that I had mastered the art of food creation. Today, this same passion prevails—only this time, my focus is to become a perfect conduit for spiritual essence to deliver to those people who ask for them the steps that will expand their consciousness to embrace their soul's evolution while opening them to the experiences of personal, firsthand spiritual experiences that tell them they are *not only human beings, but soul and spiritual beings as well.*

And last, my intention is to make this book one of the most important you'll ever read on how to accelerate the evolutionary process of your soul. Onward and upward!

Many blessings,
Walter C. Hurd

Authors note

A few people have had a question about the writing exercises in chapter three. They didn't want to stop reading to do the writing exercises, but they didn't know if it's important to complete the exercises before moving on. Not being sure what to do they simply stopped. The answer? It's up to you. If you are inspired and want to dive right in with the writing, then go ahead. But if you're inspired by what you've read and want more, then continue to the end of the book, and complete the writing after. Either answer is the right answer.

Part I
What You Can Learn from a Spiritual Master

1

What I Learned from a Spiritual Master

After high school, I couldn't go to college—because I couldn't read. I was terribly dyslexic. No one seemed to care. My parents didn't understand; they believed I was stupid. The schools in my hometown of Chagrin Falls, Ohio, didn't know what to do with me, so they just moved me along. Truthfully, I didn't much care either. My future was very clear to me, and I had a plan. More than that, I had complete trust and faith that my plan was the right one. I had a burning desire to know all there is to know about the nature of human nature, and my instincts told me that life would be my college. So, for the next six years, I traveled across America, learning about people from people.

In every place where I landed—from Ann Arbor to Aspen to Southern California—finding work that put me in conversation with a lot of people was easy. Restaurants always need help, so I waited tables and tended bar. Back in the 1960s, the tips easily covered my living expenses, and then some. Plus, restaurants offered a meal with each shift. So I would settle in for seven, eight, maybe even ten months, meet people, make friends, form relationships, and learn about the nature of human nature.

My last temporary job was as a maître d' for Harvey's Resort Hotel in Lake Tahoe, where for the first time, I found myself in a serious relationship that was impossible for me to leave, literally. I had just turned twenty-four. Oh, sure, I tried to leave—but it's a funny thing, that love in the heart. After driving less than five miles away from my "ex" girlfriend, I found myself at a pay phone, telling her I couldn't go on without her. She cried and cried.

Our love now deepened, our relationship reached a new level of commitment. To celebrate our new beginning, we found jobs in San Francisco. I worked tending bar (still studying people), and she worked as a food server. We moved into a small studio apartment in Sausalito. It was high up on a hill on what was once a huge private estate. The view of the San Francisco Bay, Golden Gate Bridge, and the city itself was amazing. Life was really good.

Ten months later, I found myself at the same window where I had so many times stood in awe of what I was seeing and appreciating the beautiful life I was privileged to live. But this cold, foggy August morning was different. I was different. I had been aware that something was wrong for some time, but this particular morning as I took in the vista, a dark, heavy feeling took hold. I felt empty and trapped. Even the landscape looked gloomy. As I observed my feelings sinking into a darker and darker place, a single thought stood out clearly in my mind: "This must be what depression is."

How long I stood there observing this new sensation, I can't say. My mind was calm, taking it all in moment by moment. As I turned to leave, another thought came into my mind loud and clear: "I *know* there is more to life than this."

AN OLD BOOK, SOME NEW BOOKS, A PHONE BOOK

The next day, I was cleaning out my traveling suitcase, the one I had used since leaving Ohio. In one of the pockets was a small book I had carried around for years. I couldn't even remember who had given it to me. That book was *Siddhartha*, by Hermann Hesse. In it was a word I had never heard but that really got my attention: *meditation*. I went to the nearest bookstore, looking for more information. There, I found a few titles about yoga. Leafing through the pictures of the exotic postures, my dark mood gone, I was inspired! I knew I had to experience what the books were promising.

This was so long ago that, although it may be hard to imagine, there was no category for yoga or meditation in the Marin County Yellow Pages. The San Francisco Yellow Pages had a small listing of about four businesses listed under *Yoga*. Walt Baptiste's name popped out. Ten days later, I took my first yoga lesson with the man who was to become my guru. It was four thirty in the afternoon on a Monday, and only one other student besides me was in attendance at the scheduled class. But that did not stop the teacher from teaching.

A man who appeared to be in his early fifties, Walt Baptiste had a cleanly shaven head, intelligent eyes, and an astonishingly muscular body. But beyond all this, there was something more. Walt Baptiste had a peaceful, yet joyful, loving presence that was *very* compelling.

Masters recognize the people with whom they will be working closely and often give them an initiatory experience—that is, an experience after which the student will never be the same again. Mine came toward the end of not just my first class but my next two classes as well, when I was blessed with indescribable spiritual experiences. Each time, I was in seated posture. As the ecstasy subsided, I heard Walt say, "Please lie on your back." As I reclined, I heard my mind's voice, loud and clear, saying, "God does exist." I knew it, and no one could ever convince me otherwise. Next came an overwhelming knowing that the man at the front of the room had created this experience for me.

I was soon to learn that, aside from being a fully realized spiritual master, Walt was also a man of the world. He knew the laws of material success and proved it to the world over and over. He won the Mr. America title in 1949 while amassing a fortune in the body-building industry. He was also an inventor, a businessman, a property developer, a magazine publisher, and a healer. It didn't take long before I understood that Walt Baptiste actually knew everything about the nature of human nature, including the soul and spiritual nature of ourselves. With that realization, I became a devoted student. I was home.

I was hooked—and taking three yoga classes a week at Walt's studio soon became a habit. I did not learn until much later just how unique his form of instruction was. Walt would guide his students into postures and talk to us while we remained in them, his words of wisdom made all the more salient because we were in the most receptive mode possible to take them in.

Walt Baptiste was a very practical master. Apart from his muscular build, there was nothing about his appearance that set him apart from the average person. He sported no long beard; he wore no robes. He spoke in plain, clear English, using no fancy intellectual verbiage in his daily communication or in his yoga or meditation classes. He seldom spoke about spirits or spirit worlds or angels or invisible guides. His focus was primarily on each individual's spiritual growth and how to keep it growing on a daily basis. His priority, too, was the introduction into each of our lives the idea of life's ultimate goals: a developed relationship with Spirit and the recognition that God is a part of ourselves, inside each of us as well as within all things and beings, just waiting to be recognized by personal, firsthand experience.

Walt Baptiste also emphasized that one of his aims was for his students to discover, through experience, their soul nature—and that to do so meant uncovering their unique and authentic nature. He pointed out that all goals of spiritual growth and soul fulfillment are attainable through a fourfold path: yoga, meditation, aggressive body conditioning, and a healthy, nutritional diet. Of course, he emphasized, these four pillars of action must be preceded by a deep, heartfelt passion for the goals of soul realization and spiritual union.

To my knowledge, Walt left little in writing, but in the introduction to a slender booklet, *The Teachings of Walt Baptiste*, which lays out in beautiful language the goals of spiritual development, he wrote: "The only 'happiness' is realized in a person when that person knows that within one Self one is growing, expanding in and through common dimension in a *living process* of Self Unfoldment." The first time I read, "A living process," I thought, *Hmm, I wonder what he means?*

Later in that work, he wrote: "The mystic aim of *living religion* is to liberate the Soul from its gross material dungeon-like encumbrance." (*"Living religion?" Here's the same idea! What could he mean by a, "living religion"?*)

He also wrote: "The Master-Guide comes to consciously unite and exalt the lower imperfect self into the higher Nature of divine-being. Once the pure Consciousness is realized, the rule by Materiality loses its force. The Soul instead, begins to reversely rule over Materiality."

AT THE STOVE

Masters not only know who their students are; they also recognize their deep inner needs—that is, they know what life experiences will help their souls to evolve in the most rapid and complete way possible. In the next months, I began working for Walt in a capacity that was utterly new to me.

A proponent of healthy nutrition myself, in 1971, I helped Walt Baptiste open the Hungry Mouth natural-foods restaurant at the corner of Clement Street and Arguello Boulevard in the Richmond district of San Francisco. Walt's building also housed his yoga studio, his wife Magana's dance studio, a gym, and a health-food store. The restaurant seated only thirty-seven people and had a cozy, welcoming feel (its redwood tables had been hand built by the young man who had been the only other participant in my initial yoga class) and great food that immediately attracted a devoted following. In fact, the Hungry Mouth attracted numerous regular customers from San Francisco Ballet dancers and UCSF medical students to Donald Sutherland, Jerry Garcia, Joan Baez, Jay Leno, Van Morrison, David Carradine (complete with an eye-catching entourage), Robin Williams (who was polishing a stand-up routine at a club down the street), and various other San Francisco legends, who found a second home of sorts at this authentic, low-key venue.

The "old" me longed to be out front, meeting and greeting, serving food, talking with everyone and learning what I could about their life experiences. But, although at first I did everything I could to avoid it, I ended up assuming the new role that Walt had very thoughtfully chosen for me. The "new" me was a cook, in training to be a chef.

Working in a hot kitchen for a spiritual master was, to say the least, not easy. I worked about a hundred hours a week, seven days a week, for three and a half years; and for the next nine and a half years, I worked between eighty and ninety five hours per week. As intense as those hours were, they were very good for me. I, like all humans, had at times let myself become addicted to distraction in my life, but I tell you that it is not possible to be distracted at the stove—especially when cooking large quantities of a variety of foods that must be perfectly timed and still produce the kind of tasty nourishment our clientele had come to expect. With that kind of intensity, I had no choice but to build a more refined focus. Because it was so good for me, I dove in, cooked and cooked, and gave it my all for the next thirteen years.

Because I, like my colleagues, had been placed where I was most likely to grow, I blossomed each day into more of my own authentic nature. During my time at the stove, I had many beautiful and meaningful experiences. There was a kind of washing away of all of the negatives of my past. Layer upon layer of anger and reactivity was surrendered; childhood wounds were healed as I worked. At the same time, I was developing a powerful inner strength and confidence. During this time, there were two very specific experiences without which I wouldn't be writing this book today.

The first of those life-changing experiences took place one night when our small restaurant was crazy busy. I was working like mad, trying to stay ahead of the orders, when, out of the corner of my eye, I saw our dishwasher come out of the dish room and walk through the kitchen, white as a sheet. He simply said two words: "I'm sick." To the right of the stove was a small window that opened to the seating area and main entrance. As I watched through that window, I saw the young man close the front door, walking away, and just then, I saw Walt step through the side entrance, walk straight through the kitchen without a word, and enter the dishwashing room.

Now I knew he understood what was happening, but I still felt the need to say something, so I went to the door of the dish room. There Walt stood in white shoes, pure white pants, and a white shirt. He rolled up his sleeves and said, "I'll take care of this. You get the orders out." I wasn't in a position to argue, but still, it just didn't feel right that he had to wash pots and dishes.

Next, I brought my guru a stack of sauté pans to scrub, but before I could turn around and get back to the stove, Walt began to speak to me in a slow, calm, hum-drummy kind of voice. "You know, Walter," he began, "I've been wanting to mention something to you…I want you to try more to…"

I was thinking, *Whhhaaatt? Now?* I couldn't possibly show Walt disrespect by asking him to stop talking, but at the same time, there were a bunch of orders waiting to be cooked. I thought, *I'll just wait until he pauses to breathe.* But he never stopped talking! I finally got a chance to jump in between Walt's sentences and remind him about the orders.

"Walter, yes," he said, "Get those orders out!" (His tone implied, "*What are you standing there for?*")

The next time I took a stack of sauté pans back to be cleaned, *he did it again*! This time I didn't wait; I reminded him of the orders. "Oh, yes, Walter. Get those orders out." He said it with that same, "*What are you standing there for?*" tone. On my way back to the stove, I thought, *I am not going back there again.* A short time later an order came in for three orders of a dish called Japanese-Style Fish and Prawns. There was only one pot big enough to prep three orders in, and it was in the dish room on a shelf near the door. I also knew the pot was clean, so I decided to dart in there and grab it fast, thinking maybe I'd get away before Walt said anything.

In the dish room, I quickly made a grab for the pan and spun around, but just as I reached the door, I heard, "Walter!" I turned around, and there Walt was, wearing a huge smile and shaking the water out of a large soup pot. Then, in a loud, firm voice, he said, "My job is to accelerate your evolution."

I was so stunned, I didn't know what to say. So I think I just said, "OK, thanks!"

Once at the stove again, I tried to process what had happened. I thought, *What an amazing piece of information to have! What an incredible understanding about why I'm here.* Of course, I had no real idea what he was talking about at the time. But I do know today, because I have lived his words for many years—and so can you!

FOLLOW THE RECIPE

The second life-changing lesson began two weeks before the restaurant was scheduled to open. It was small enough that it only took three of us working full time to run it: two people in the front doing the serving, and me at the stove. Walt wanted all three of us to learn to prepare the menu items, so one morning, we gathered in the kitchen, and he handed us each a copy of the menu. It was huge. There were twenty-two main dish items: eleven meat and eleven vegetarian. There was a list of sandwiches, six dinner salads, health shakes, and desserts. Everything, even the desserts, was to be made to order.

Walt trained us until opening day and then stayed with us during the busy periods for six more weeks. One evening during cleanup, he again gathered us in the kitchen. He assured us that we were doing a great job and that he felt confident we could carry on without him. He told us he was leaving for a month. "But before I go," he said, "I just want to make sure you understand one very important thing. Whatever you do, don't change the recipes. Can you all agree to that?"

It seemed easy enough to agree to keep on making the dishes the way he'd taught us, and we all readily agreed. "Yeah, sure, Walt, no problem." So he left.

He came back a month later, walked right into the kitchen where the three of us were gathered together, uncovered a pot simmering on the stove, and said, "I want to taste what's in this." He did and immediately asked, "Who changed this recipe?" Luckily, it wasn't me. "I told you," he said, "don't change the recipes." A few weeks later, the same thing: Walt came in unannounced, went right up to the stove, tasted a dish. "Who made this?" Again, thank heavens, not me. Again, "I *told* you, *don't change the recipes.*"

Over the course of the next year, Walt's sixth sense about altered recipes proved uncannily reliable. Every single time he insisted on tasting a suspect pot, it turned out to be a recipe with, shall we say, some improvisations. Over and over, he would admonish us with the same words: "Now, don't change the recipe."

Finally, one night, after Walt let out a particularly loud (*scary* might be more accurate) and irritable, "Don't change the recipe," I turned to resume cleaning the stove when it finally dawned on me: *Masters don't repeat things just to hear themselves talk. There's always a reason behind the reason for saying something.* I also thought, *He's trying to tell us about something that would happen if we followed his instructions to a tee.* I wanted to know what that was, so right there, I vowed to myself to make every dish exactly as he showed us, every single time, for as long as I was there. Interestingly, that was the last time he checked to make sure we were following his recipes.

During the next twelve years, that's precisely what I did—and a strange thing happened: The food got better and better and better. Now, how can that be? If you're replicating a recipe exactly the same way every time, how can the quality steadily, increasingly improve? A big part of the answer: it's in the nuances.

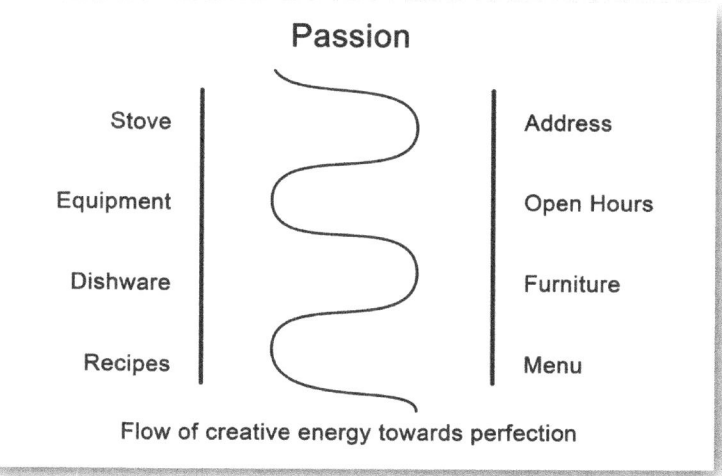

Let me explain: to be successful in any creative endeavor, you must establish three conditions. The first—without which everything else is a waste of time and energy—is *passion*. You must have a deep, passionate reason for doing what you are doing. The second condition is a *structure*. For example, the structure for creating food in a restaurant is the location of the business, its hours of operation, its equipment, (refrigerator, stove, pots and pans, and so on), its menu items, its order board, and its recipes. All these items are stationary and permanent. The third thing you must have is a *flow of creative energy* through the structure—creative energy that is directly related to why you created the structure in the first place: because of your passion, your desire.

What flowed through the structure of Walt's recipes were learning patterns that involved discovering the nuances of the food that I was making. Take, for instance, one of our most popular dishes, Hawaiian-Style Prawns. The recipe was, "In heated oil, seasoned with garlic, salt, pepper, and curry powder, sauté prawns. When the sautéing is done, at high heat, add butter, a little water, and fresh-cut pineapple. Cover, and turn the heat down." But note how many nuances are concealed in this seemingly simple formula. How high is the flame by which you heat the oil? How much salt, how much pepper, and curry powder do you use? How long do you sauté the prawns so that they are not underdone or overcooked? How much water and butter do you add? How much pineapple? When you put the lid on, how far do you lower the heat? If the temperature is too low, the flavors don't blend; too high, and the dish takes on a kind of bitter under-taste. For years, I worked on refining the nuances of every single dish on the entire menu—and the food got better and better and better, still based on the same recipes.

But that's not all. There are many kinds of learning patterns created by the energy passing through a structure. There came a time when I had to give more of myself. I was led to understand that I needed to pay attention to what I was thinking and feeling while I was doing the cooking, because a chef's mood also goes into the food.

The way I learned this was the same way I learned everything: through experience. I was usually the guy who came in first thing in the morning and the last to leave at night. But I did get a two-hour break in the middle of the afternoon. I would go upstairs to work out in the gym, then go to the yoga room to practice yoga and meditate, and then go back to the kitchen. If I had an outrageously good meditation and workout, it almost never failed that a few hours later, one of our food servers would say something like, "Hey, what are you doing back there? People are raving about the food!" A similar thing would happen on days when I looked out through the small window in the kitchen and felt an immense rush of affection for our diners. In connecting with spiritual essence in meditation or breathing with a rush of affection for people around me, I was "in love" with what was in the pan in front of me. That love would, literally, become an ingredient in any dish I was preparing. Again, year after year, the food improved. As I now understand it, this was because the level of vibration in the food grew higher and higher.

There came a time, somewhere in the eleventh year, that my own instincts told me I needed to seek the *perfect expression* of what it was that I was making. To do that, I had to become an open conduit for the flow of spiritual energy to pass through me and into the food. The results were beautiful and amazing. With my practice, the food took off to a whole new level of quality.

I had never before really had the experience of truly mastering something, but toward the end of my time at the restaurant, I realized that this is what I had done. By this time, we were up to four on the kitchen staff. Walt came in one day, suggesting we come up with a daily special that would not only entice customers but also give us a chance to be a little creative. That creativity came to me in leaps and bounds. In the afternoon when I was prepping for the evening, I would run out to the storage shed to get a single ingredient I needed, and as soon as I stepped through the door, all of these recipes would flood into my brain. And the ingredients I needed to create whichever one I chose were right there on the shelves. Instead of returning to the kitchen with one item, I had an armload of stuff. This happened fairly frequently, but I didn't think much about it at first—until the day Walt came in early in the morning before anyone else was there and said, "Walter, your food has taken on a whole new dimension. You know that, right?"

I didn't know what to say. I think I said, "Thank you," or something like that.

And then, as he turned to walk out, he said, "You know, I think you've mastered this thing."

That's the first time I had that idea, that concept of mastery, in my mind. But, in a way, I knew exactly what he meant, because I had already experienced what it means to master something. What does it mean to master something? Mastery of anything has to do with a very particular event. I have come to see that it means creating something in the course of a process that has moments of the miraculous about it.

I think I was waiting to hear that acknowledgment from Walt. A few months after that, I left.

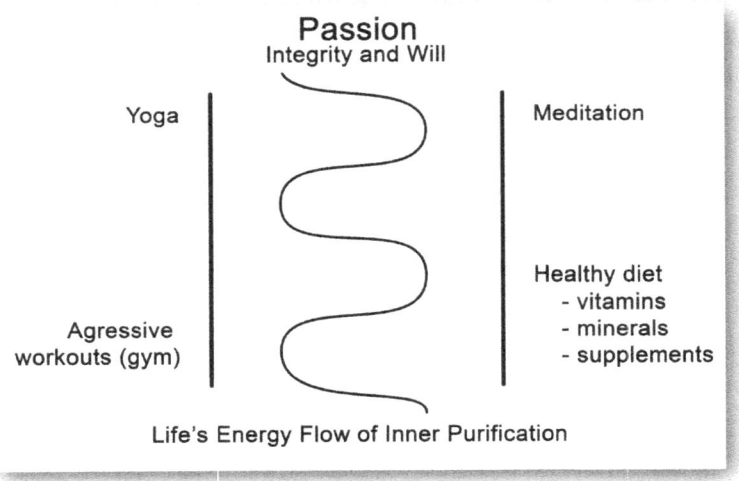

So the question now is: what form did Walt Baptiste create because of his passion for our souls' evolution and spiritual growth? His structure was made of four specific disciplines: yoga, meditation, proactive health-building exercises (gym workouts), and a healthy diet that included vitamin and mineral supplements.

There is something very interesting about this form. These aren't structural conditions that are immovable; they're actually disciplines that allow for a great deal of individual discovery. So how can you create this form to start the free flow of creative energy within your life? You have to add your deep, heartfelt passion for spiritual growth or soul fulfillment. And you must add two other character qualities. One is a steadfast, everyday integrity for implementing the four disciplines (in other words, be consistent), and the second is a strong will to do what you have chosen to do.

Each discipline feeds the other. Yoga is the great healer that creates space within you. That's why after a yoga class, you can feel really calm and relaxed and yet at the same time energized. The space created by the healing was filled by higher life energy.

Meditation develops personal will in a natural way, but the intention of meditation is spiritual growth. Meditation draws spiritual essence into you. Because space is created for it through yoga healing, spiritual essence is invited in to become a part of you. But there's a problem: this spiritual energy's rate of vibration is slightly higher than your current rate of vibration as a being, and the body needs energy to integrate the new intensities of spiritual essences—which it gets through body conditioning. That's why we strengthen the body in the gym. Walt once wrote, "Meditation without body conditioning becomes a violence to the body." Healthy eating and vitamin and mineral supplements also feed the body in its ability to integrate this higher rate of vibration, the result of yoga and meditation.

With all the principles in place, energy flows through the form directly related to why you've built the form. And what will happen in your life because of Walt's form and your sincere commitment? The same thing that happened to me at the stove: you will experience periods of letting go, in a very natural way, of your negative past. You will also experience synchronistic life events—*daily*—that tell you who you are and what your authentic nature is. This will happen day after day, month after month, year after year, for your entire life-span. And your consciousness will grow, expanding in intelligence and wisdom. This is what Walt Baptiste meant by "a living process."

The person you would have been at death had you not followed these principles would be very different from the person you *will* be if you live the Path of the Masters, as Walt Baptiste called it, with all of its rich personal experiences.

ABOVE THE WORLD

When I left the restaurant, my intense desire for spiritual growth was still intact. I took with me the four life-affirming pillars that Walt had provided. I also took the qualities of integrity and will that allowed me to stay consistent and disciplined within his structure.

Every single day, I practiced what Walt had taught me. And, as anyone who practices these things does, I continued to have periods of letting go of the negative energies of my past. As a result, I felt my life moving both forward and upward. I also had countless little (and sometimes big), miraculous synchronistic moments every day of finding myself in exactly the right place at the right time in order for my learning to continue. Of course, none of this stopped life's inevitable ups and downs from occurring.

One of the practical reasons I stopped working at Walt's restaurant was that during my years there, I had married, and now my wife and I were raising three children. I desperately wanted to spend more time with my family, and restaurant work is not conducive to that. To resolve that problem, my wife and I made a plan: instead of working long hours at the Hungry Mouth, I would take a restaurant job working only nights and weekends, using my days to find a nine-to-five job. We figured that at the very most, this would take a year. So…three years went by, and I was still working nights and weekends at a restaurant.

At this point, I was filled with frustration because none of the day jobs I applied for had worked out. Things reached a point when I had to have a conversation with myself and ask why. I realized that at Walt's restaurant, I had been doing exactly the right thing at the right time and place out of who I was. And now, it turned out that on an unconscious level, I was trying to recreate that dynamic again, but with no luck. I didn't know how to solve my problem. I only knew—again, on some deep level—that my time with Walt Baptiste had been a great training for something else, something very specific that I had to do, and I wanted to know what that was! The question in my mind, growing louder and louder, now became: *Why was I really born?*

Then, one day, I was heading off to work for my evening shift in the restaurant, leaving home early so I could stop and get a coffee in a café that I liked. I had a cup in my hand and was about to take a seat when, just before my bottom hit the chair—well, all I can say is, I was gone. In a blink of an eye, a part of me was somehow above the world, gazing down on it. There was a guide beside me, and what we were looking at was what I can only describe as *the deep, unconscious need of the human population at that moment in history.* We were taking a read on it. Then I was "back." The whole event happened so quickly that I am sure it didn't look to anyone else in that café like anything out of the ordinary had occurred. But my lingering image of hovering over the world was crystal clear. Here's the best part: when I came back, my head was filled with a whole new understanding. Over the years, I'd had experiences—while working at the stove and after leaving the restaurant—that appeared to be unrelated to one another. But when I came back, I was given to see that these experiences composed one cohesive, complete set of principles. And along with this understanding came all the nuances of those principles. So, I had this massive amount of new information in my head.

I went to work and finished out my shift, feeling as though I was about to burst. I had this incredible wealth of information, and I wanted to share it with my wife—because *this was it*, the reason I was born—and I knew it. I raced home to tell her what had happened.

But, as I immediately discovered, this wasn't going to be so easy.

2

Mastering Life

"Walter, Walter, please stop," my wife said, her brow furrowed. "Stop it. I can't understand a word you're saying."

I had bounded into our living room, letting loose a flood of the new information I was so eager to explain. But it wasn't going as planned. "Oh, oh, I'm sorry," I said, "I'm just really excited. Let me sleep on it. I'll tell you tomorrow."

The next morning, I started in again, and my wife said, "Walter, you've got to stop. This is crazy! I can't understand a word." If I reverted back to talking about everyday stuff, no problem. But the moment I talked again about the experience I'd had, I apparently didn't make any sense. I waited a few weeks and tried again, but now my wife said, "You're scaring me. Just cut it out."

Somewhere along the line, a friend suggested I write everything down. "It's still scattered in the ether. There's no linear order to it, and we need to see that order to make sense of it," she said. So, for the next six months, I sat down every day and, as best I could, put everything in an order. What appeared was a "seminar" of sorts. Three friends volunteered to let me deliver it to them on a Saturday. In all, the whole program took six hours.

Part of the seminar had to do with writing and, as one of the women there was writing, I looked over and saw her eyes tearing up. The next thing I knew, tears were streaming down her cheeks. I thought, "Gee whiz. To be touched this way! This is...*interesting*."

I met with the same three people two weeks afterward, and all of them told me that the seminar had really impacted their lives. "I'm thinking about myself in a different way," one of them said. A short time later, another friend asked me to give him the class, and the same thing happened—minus the tears. Suddenly, he was very serious about his life in ways he hadn't been before. When that happened, I thought, *OK, this is it! This is everything I wanted. I know exactly who I am, and I know why I'm here.* And I knew exactly what to do. I could see it on the horizon right over there, and I was bursting with readiness to take off toward it.

YANKED BY THE COLLAR

But then… Have you ever had an experience when you're going one way and you can see the path very clearly—and then life comes along and grabs the back of your collar and yanks so hard, your feet go up in the air and you're on your back, looking at the sky and wondering what happened? Well, that happened to me. Specifically, I lost my wife and children to divorce.

Divorce was the most painful, challenging thing I had ever experienced. It was especially hard because my wife and I still loved each other. We just couldn't live in harmony any longer. There were even times when we had to help each other through—when she was strong and resolute, I was weak, and vice versa.

Manhood is a funny thing. Facing what comes to us, positive or negative, as men, strengthens our characters. Divorce had come to me, and I was determined to face it gracefully. But in truth, emotionally, I was devastated—a real emotional wreck. It was a full year before I began to find my footing. It was four years before I began to have some feeling for life again. Thank God, I had a job to throw myself into. The distractions seemed to work as my divorce therapy. But during my time off, I was often anxious, feeling lost or sad—really sad.

After about a year, I found myself in the downtown area of Walnut Creek, California. I had bought something in a store and returned to my car, which was parked by the curb. I put my key in the ignition, but I didn't turn it on. Instead, I found myself staring, with one of those glazed-over, subconscious gazes, out the windshield. I'm sure I looked strange to the people walking by, but I didn't see them. My mind was turning over in a subconscious rant, thinking and thinking and thinking. When I began to observe my thoughts, I realized that I was thinking about my ex-wife and listing all the ways she had acted toward me that made me not want to be in our marriage anymore. But then I realized, "Well, wait a minute. She has *her* list of things that *I* did that made *her* want to leave the marriage." I knew what they were—she had certainly told me often enough—so I started listing them, one after the other. The aha moment came when I realized that the whole list of negative attitudes and responses I'd brought into our marriage had developed out of experiences I had witnessed or experienced myself as a child growing up in an extremely abusive home environment. It was a real eye-opener to realize that I had duplicated the same dark home atmosphere I had so determinedly escaped from when I was eighteen.

And in that realization, I made the decision that I would *never* enter into any relationship while still holding the memories that were such a negative creative force within me. So, I made a vow right then and there: I was not going to stop until all of those negatively charged memories were healed—*all of them—not one negative emotion left.* And why wouldn't I make such a vow? After all, I knew all the principles. I had been given them in my "above the world" experience and at the stove. So my vow became my full-time focus, my reason for life.

And for eight years, my life went *straight downhill!*

During those eight years, life was one big, confusing struggle. I never made enough money to rent my own apartment, so I either rented a room in someone's house or shared an apartment. Anytime I got myself into that kind of situation, after a few months, maybe eight or ten, I had to leave. Things went bad for all kinds of reasons: there was one super control freak who was in my business all the time; there was a person who seemed healthy and well but suddenly began acting out-of-control crazy; there was another person who'd been sober for twelve years but one day chose to start a ten-day drinking binge.

And housing was not the worst of it. The worst had to do with money and jobs. I struggled just to earn a living for myself. No matter what decision I made, things went wrong. The longest job I had lasted for fifteen months. Every other position turned into something unexpected after I'd started. One company shut down a number of its stores, one of which was mine. Another time, my hours were suddenly cut in half, and I couldn't live on the resulting salary. Another time, I was told I would be doing *this*, but it turned out that I was also expected to do *that*—which I wasn't qualified to do and wasn't paid for—so I had to leave. Job after job failed to meet my needs. I was in that part of my life's lesson where there was no energy, no intelligence to guide me to the right job, no flow of energy that allowed life to deliver what I needed.

At my lowest point, I found myself all too often talking on the phone with bill collectors. At first, I tried to find out the rules of their game. Just how much would it take for them to recognize that whatever I promised, I would deliver? But then, why play the game? "No," I told myself firmly out of frustration, "*get a job* that pays your bills and living expenses!"

But here's the deal: this isn't an "oh, pity poor Walter" story. Not at all; not even close. I was well trained. I had Walt Baptiste's form, which I kept up. I still practiced, on a daily basis, yoga, meditation, workouts at the gym, and healthful eating. Also, I knew, because I had learned while working in the Hungry Mouth at the stove a long, long time ago, that everything—*everything*—moves in cycles.

CYCLES OF LIFE

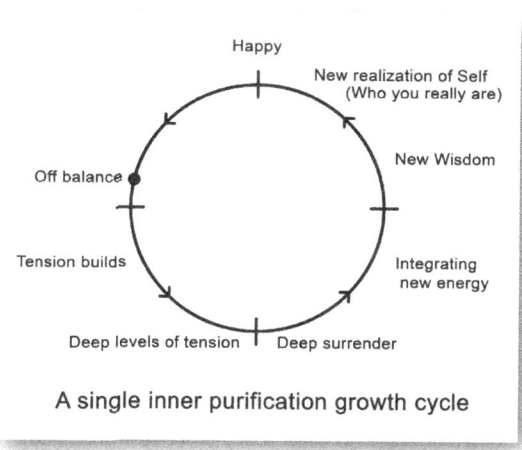

A single inner purification growth cycle

Let me explain what I mean. Above is a simplified chart of the cycles of inner purification and spiritual growth. Starting at the top, we're going along and everything's just beautiful. We're happy. We're having fun. As we come down the left side of the circle, something happens, and we're thrown off balance. We don't feel quite as good as we used to. The reasons for this are primarily on the subconscious level. As we move down the arc even further, approaching the bottom point of the circle, tensions grow—although, again, we don't necessarily know why. All we know is that we are angry, or we're frustrated, or we're frightened like crazy. The tension increases more and more until we hit bottom and, after we've been holding so much tension for so long, we simply cannot hold it any longer, and we let go. At this point, we are *very* tired, both emotionally and physically. So when we let go, we surrender our subconsciously held tensions—involving some elements of our past, so completely, so deeply, that the energy field that has been in tension reduces in size. And in that deep, powerful release, spiritual energy enters, filling the space that was opened up by our surrender. (After all, this is what we are: material form and spiritual energy.)

Now, spiritual energy, which is a higher energy, a higher life force, enters into our organism, our state of being. But the body and the emotions and the subconscious need time to integrate this energy. We need time to understand and integrate all this new energy that brings with it an understanding of the nature of our original problem. As we approach the top again, beautiful things begin to happen. On the conscious level, if we're looking for clarity, we have amazing insights into what the original problem was all about—what it *really* was all about. We gain truths about our circumstances, truths about the nature of being human, and truths about life itself—one after the other. Walt Baptiste used to call this "the sifting of the real from the unreal." As a result, we become happier…happier…and happier, until we are at the very top of the cycle again.

These cycles occur in the subconscious for almost everyone, but those who have a heightened self-awareness—and especially those who work in an environment with a spiritual master—feel the cycles in their lives and become very familiar with them. So, during my very long downturn, all I did was keep up my practices and watch these cycles. It got so that when I found myself at the bottom of a cycle, holding severe levels of tension, I would think, *This is great*, because I knew I would come out into the upturn sooner or later. Sometimes I'd wake up at one in the morning, filled with anger, the muscles in my body hard as steel, and I would literally think, *This is great! I get* to *heal the cause of this anger: to grow, to mature, to evolve a little more*—around and around and around. I also knew that each downturn couldn't last forever. I knew that at some point, it would turn around, and I was watching for it, waiting for it. Of course, some downturns went on far longer than I wanted them to, but that's the way it happened.

ENOUGH!

At one point, I found what I thought was a good, secure job. It was with a small, family-owned business. It had existed for a long, long time, and it paid me well. The only little red flag was that the owners were talking about selling and retiring one day. No problem. For now, I had enough money to get my own apartment. I was so happy about that. I was so proud when I paid the deposits and first month's rent. Finally, a place of my very own! Well, one morning, I was heading to work—walking because my car wasn't doing so well—and when I got there, I found a padlock and a sign on the door: *Lost Our Lease, Out of Business.* Underneath was a letter thanking the customers for their patronage.

I was stunned. I went home feeling the old, familiar high levels of frustration. It took several hours to settle down, but I wasn't about to waste time. With résumés in hand, I made the by now all-too-familiar rounds, but I got no's everywhere. Two weeks later, my rent was due, and I didn't have the money for it. My car was in the carport, broken—no brakes, no generator, dead battery. I woke up and tried to shake off all my angst and fear by taking a shower. I got dressed and headed for the door, planning to go to this little coffee shop down the street. But I didn't get to the door. Instead, I paced back and forth. I wasn't even aware I was pacing. All I was aware of was that I was thinking about something, though I didn't really know quite what it was. Next, I became aware that I was staring down at the carpet, just standing there, looking at this one spot—and my mind was thinking about who I had been when I worked back at Walt Baptiste's restaurant. *What the hell? What happened?* I was comparing that person with the person I was now experiencing—huge difference! And I was thinking,

This can't be. What happened to that powerful, confident man? And out of that question, suddenly, I had this little fleeting thought: *That person's still right here. He's still inside you.*

And right then, as I had this one, small thought, I felt this unbelievable amount of energy raising right out of my gut, past my solar plexus, up into my heart, and into my throat. And I screamed uncontrollably at the top of my voice, "*Enough!*"

UPTURN

Man, did I feel good after that. I felt fantastic. There was a light, tingling sensation in every cell of my body. It felt as though a huge weight had been lifted from my shoulders. I could breathe like I hadn't taken a breath in years. I left my apartment, still enjoying the high. As I slid the key in to lock the door, in that very moment, I had this powerful knowing: *Absolutely everything's going to be just fine.*

I walked toward my usual café—the coffee wasn't so great, but it was cheap—and passed this other, very popular European-style café-restaurant where the coffee cost more but was really delicious. I thought about my usual place: *Nope, not this morning. Time to celebrate.* I turned into the popular café. As I entered, the owner stepped out from the kitchen and exclaimed loudly, "Walter! Where have you been? I need a manager. I've been looking for you." I had talked to her some weeks back, and she knew I was job hunting. So we had a little meeting—and I started work the next morning. This time, I was secure in the "knowing" that this job was the *right* one.

A couple of days went by. A friend of mine walked into the café. He said, "Walter, you're working here!"

I said, "Yeah, life is great again. I'm making enough of a salary to keep that little apartment. Money's really tight, but I'm going to keep it. I don't want to move again. The only thing I need now is to get my car fixed, and then I'll really be good to go."

My friend said, "Oh, my cousin's a mechanic. He'll come over and help you." The cousin came over, I got the parts we needed, and he fixed the car.

So now, I had a good job, I was still in my apartment, and my car was running. I thought, *This is good. This is very good.*

A few months went by, and another friend came to visit me at work. "Walter," she said, "I have a friend I've been bugging for a long time. He has a big, beautiful house and a great big backyard with a two-room cottage on the property. He never rents it out, but I've convinced him to rent it to you." She then told me how much the rent was—about half what I was paying currently. The cottage was beautiful, with grass, tall oak trees, and flowers all around. I moved right in.

Life was definitely looking up now. A few more months passed, and another friend came into the café to ask what my days off were. I answered, "I only have one: Thursday."

She said, "OK," and she returned a few days later, announcing that on Thursday evenings, I was to go over to the house of a mutual friend and teach yoga in his backyard. (It was July, and the evening air was perfect for outdoor yoga practice.) At first, there were only about six or seven friends attending, but within a few weeks, sixteen or seventeen neighbors and friends of friends had joined us.

One night, a woman approached me after class and said, "I want you to give me private classes in my home."

I said, "Well, why don't you just keep coming to these classes?"

I explained that I had never given private classes before, but she insisted. "No, you *are* coming to my house, and you *are* giving me classes. I've been diagnosed with cancer, and I know you can help me."

The idea was totally new to me. I really had no idea how I could help this woman with her cancer. Again, I started to decline. "You know, I don't…"

She cut me off midsentence: "You *are* coming to my house, and you *are* giving me classes. And I'm going to *pay you*."

"OK, I'm coming to your house."

After I gave her four classes, her husband saw how she was changing and wanted to get in on the action. So I began teaching the two of them. To this day, I still don't know what happened with her cancer. All I know is that she stopped the classes. She never showed any signs of being sick, and I never again heard her mention anything about treatments. I felt it would be too personal to ask about it, but my guess is that she had been misdiagnosed.

As it turned out, it was her husband who had real problems. He was holding massive amounts of tension around the midsection of his body: dark, negative tension that had been building up for years. The method of cracking and finally dissolving his self-shielding tension was by no means easy for him. It involved sitting in very uncomfortable yoga postures while forcefully breathing a series of rapid yogic breaths. Two, sometimes three times a week, we worked. The energy lifting off of him was so dark and nasty, I had to be sure not to stand too close so I could avoid being unpleasantly affected by it.

But this man was his own hero. Within ten months, he was a completely different person: tons of new energy, streams of light emanating from his eyes. He happily and animatedly described doing all the things he'd wanted to do but had put off for years. One morning, his wife surprised me with a phone call. Laughingly, she asked, "What are you doing to him?" Apparently, he wouldn't stop chasing her around the kitchen.

Friends of his, seeing his new attitude and energy, began asking how it had happened. When he told them, "Oh, I've got this guy…"people began calling me to set appointments.

BUILDING A FORM

Our experience together was very good for me. I'd leave a session and wonder: how had I known the exact postures he needed for healing? I was operating strictly by instinct, but there was no denying the effect. People calling for appointments offered more confirmation that I was adept in my ability to help others. In a very natural way, a new vocation had come to me.

In the coming years, I worked with a lot of people, and with every kind of problem: physical, emotional, psychological. I didn't care what anyone's problems were, because I knew I could help them. The question is, how did I help them? I'm not educated; I never went to college. But the answer is really quite simple. I built a form.

Building a form was easy because the first condition (or principle) was in place: these people had a passionate desire to heal themselves. They were sick and tired of being sick. The second principle was their commitment to attending meetings with me. The third (you really only need three, though four is best) evolved because, as I start working with people, I ask them to talk about themselves. As they do, sooner or later, they say something that is vitally important about their problem—without understanding the importance of their words. I'll stop them and ask, "Hey, do you realize what you just said?" As I point out how their comment relates to their issue, I'll have them write it down. This often happens two or three times in each session. Sometimes, during a really good session, it happens a lot. And it isn't long before they see the insights they glean by writing, so they bring their notebooks to every meeting. In fact, they often start writing before I even point something out to them. So now, we have three principles' to our form: desire, commitment and writing.

I have always tried to get that fourth leg of the form in there. People heal faster if I can find it. Finding what works has to do with what each person is naturally inclined to. Most men love working the body, so I'd take them to the gym. That was easy. With women, I had to find out what they related to, something they had a motivating desire to do to break up their mental and emotional patterns. With some it was yoga, but not always. One woman had been a dancer as a teenager and started dancing again; another woman was a runner. She could no longer run, but she began walking two hours a week.

Simultaneously, during my beginning period of working privately with people, a very interesting thing was happening to me. I was changing inside; I was becoming a very different person. I had been sensing this even before I'd encountered that "Out of Business" note on the door, but now I was really feeling it. To explain to you what I mean by this, I need to give you a super-ultra crash course in what is known as the chakra system.

A CHAKRA PRIMER

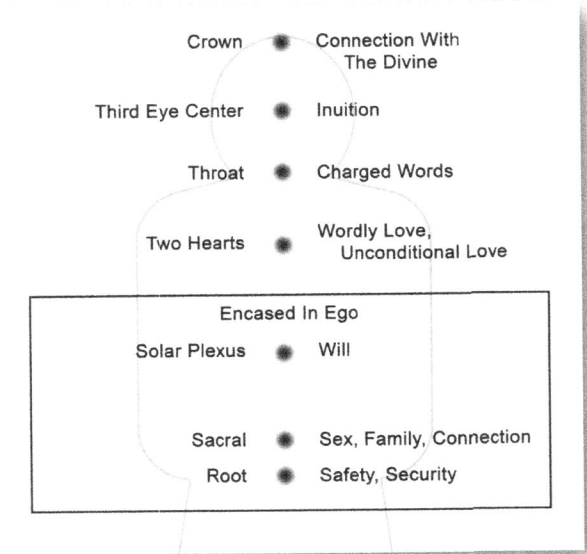

The subject of chakras is complex. There are ancient texts, modern books, and even whole college courses that tackle it. But for our purposes, we only need the simplest, most basic description of the importance of the chakras in our lives.

The chakras are a series of seven etheric energy centers located along the axis of the body, from the base of the spine to the top of the head. Five of the chakras are stationed near the spine, behind the endocrine glands. One of their jobs is to send energy to the glands responsible for making hormones, but that's certainly not all they do. Another chakra is in the center of the head, between the eyebrows, in position for energizing the pineal and pituitary gland. It's the third-eye center, the "all-knowing" chakra.

Each energy center brings with it an aspect of our humanness. The force of its energy serves as an involuntary drive that causes us to act in specific ways, the totality of which makes up the nature of human nature.

The first energy center, just under the base of the spine, gives us our drive to survive: our basic need to feed ourselves, clothe ourselves, find shelter, and protect our families from danger. The second energy center supplies the force that drives us to have sex, though it has to do with more than sex. It also has everything to do with our urge to procreate—to find that perfect partner to have children with. All the spoken and unspoken laws around sex and family stem from this center. The 3rd energy center above the second gives us the *will* to create a life as we understand it; that is, as we have been educated to believe life is supposed to be based on the lower chakras. In other words, the third chakra provides the will to survive, find a mate, have and raise children, and so on.

The three lower chakras are encased in the ego. One job of the ego is to protect us by not letting us get into situations that will harm us. Another job of the ego is to drive us to seek out and find material and/or self-serving pleasure. What we feel constitute protection and pleasure is drawn from the memories of our past experiences. The ego references our history, the experiences that we've already had, as we are about to take an action. It says, "That restaurant gave us great pleasure; let's go back there," or, "This person really offended us; let's never talk to him again." So, in short, ego is about protection and pleasure, based on the past. That is why, if we are in the habit of navigating life from our subconscious mind, we wind up doing the same things over and over again, like a skipping CD.

The next energy center is the heart. We actually have two hearts. One is the human heart, which loves with condition. It says, "I'll give you my love, but I expect something in return." The other is the inner heart, the higher heart. It loves without condition; it loves just to love. (When I cook food, it is this second heart's love that is in the food itself.) The human heart can be as dark and negative about issues of love as it can be loving. It can carry anger around "heartfelt" situations. It can carry fear. It can actually carry hatred around issues of love (the reason, for example, that divorces can be so crazy).

The next center is the throat center (more about this in a minute). Above that is the "third eye" or the *ajna* center. This is the place in the middle of the forehead where spiritual energy manifests during meditation. This is the door, the receptor for our higher instincts, our intuition, our higher intelligence and wisdom. This is where the soul resides, and when we meditate daily, we open our communication with the soul. The soul comes closer, and we hear and feel its urges; we hear its thoughts.

A seventh center resides at the top of the head. It is the opening where spiritual energy passes through, energizing the brain when your meditation reaches a point of refined focus.

When the higher centers begin to energize, the effects of the ego-based centers begin to diminish. That is what was happening to me as I taught yoga. All the lower centers were still there if I needed them, but now by conscious choice. I was no longer driven by them. I was being driven instead by the higher centers. In working with people, I was not only helping them, but was also energizing my higher chakras—all of which came out in my throat when I spoke with them.

As I worked with people, I had to be operating from my higher centers all the time, because I needed the wisdom to know what to *say* and the perfect timing to know when to say it—and that is what my intuition told me. When I saw people completely turn their lives around, my heart was overjoyed. The words passed through my throat pulsating with the energy of the higher centers, and people responded beautifully to them.

Now, for the first time, after all those years, I really understood the reasons for the practices. I was living the goals of practice: experiencing the freedom from a limited past and drawing on the power of the higher centers—the heart; the mind with its talents of insight, instincts, higher "knowing," and moral compass; and a voice that communicated from a heart that radiated that "different kind of love" that Walt Baptiste had talked about in class. It was a love that found compassion for all beings and things.

I was living the meaning of Walt Baptiste's written comments alluded to in the first chapter of this book. These types of experiences *are* a "living religion." And, as Walt said, "Once the pure Consciousness is realized, the rule by materiality loses its force. The Soul instead begins to reversely rule over materiality."

THREE WOMEN

Let me tell you about three people I worked with. One woman was very somber; she practically never smiled. She wasn't unhappy, and she wasn't sad—she was just somber. During a short conversation, I suggested meeting her privately for a few hours. She agreed, and we did some writing for three hours. She said, "Thank you very much, that was great," smiling in a way I don't think I'd ever seen.

Another woman, whom I met through a mutual friend, had lost hope; she was stuck and had been just floating through life for several years. After I asked her a few carefully chosen, interview-type questions, she said, "I think you can help me." We worked together eight times, four times a month for two months, and she said, "Thank you very much; that's all I need."

A third woman I met at a party, and as we talked, she said, "I think you can help me. I have fibromyalgia [a painful musculoskeletal disorder]. I've had it for ten years, and I'm sick of it." We started working together, and it turned out that her life was so crazy, and she was so mercurial—up and down, up and down—and doing far too many things to hurt herself. It took a whole year for her to get a hold on her emotions to the point where she would settle down enough to tackle the serious issue of her fibromyalgia. But then, four and half months later, no fibromyalgia. She too said thank you, and that was that.

The first woman wrote me a letter two months after our brief writing session. In it, she listed all the ways her life had changed because of our three hours together. One thing she told me was that she had always wanted to remodel her house. She'd even had the money saved to do it for years, but never had the courage. As she wrote the letter, her house was completely torn apart, and she said she couldn't wait to see what it was going to look like when it was finished. The second thing she told me was that she had sat down and had conversations with her two children—both of whom had been nearly estranged from her—and that their relationship had changed from one of almost constant fighting and disrespect to one where they could hardly wait to see one another.

The second woman courageously quit working at a job she should have left years earlier. The first thing she did? She said yes to the man who had been asking to marry her for five years. But that's not all. She started her own interior-design business. Twelve months later, she was immersed in, and profiting from, sixteen projects. As anyone in the interior-design business world knows, that's a huge success.

The woman with fibromyalgia who found her disease gone after four and half months of addressing it said it never came back. I see her every once in a while, and she tells me that if she ever feels it trying to come on again, she knows exactly what to do, and it vanishes. Fibromyalgia is one of these diseases of which no one knows the cause or the cure, but this was her experience.

CAN I DO THIS?

The next question I expect you might have is: What if I want to take advantage of Walt Baptiste's teachings? What would you suggest that I do?

First, you'll need to sit down and have a conversation with yourself. Ask, "Am I ready to take full responsibility for my life? "And really think about that. Full responsibility for your life means no more blaming others, no more blaming outside circumstances. *Full and complete responsibility*. If the answer is an overwhelming *yes*, then you have your passion.

If you go into the hills of Northern India, you can find many caves where monks are sitting in meditation twenty-four hours a day, every day. They do this because their goal is to achieve a perfect harmony and union with Spirit, with God. But that goal is not easy for many of us in our culture to relate to. We don't have a sense of the outcome, and so most of us find no passion there. But to discover what our soul is here to do, to find its talent and its genius, is a goal most of us *can* relate to. We want to know why we are here, and we want to live from that realization because it brings great meaning to our lives. When we know what we are meant to be doing from the soul level and we live it, we become great contributors to our loved ones and to the world at large.

So, to get back to the original question: If your answer to "Are you ready to take full and complete responsibility for your life?" is a resounding *yes*, then you are good to go.

There are some people who understand the concept of finding their purpose but still lack the passion. If this describes you, it may be that there is a part of your life that you need to pay attention to, and you may have been putting it aside for years—just like the woman who wouldn't remodel her house. You may need to find the courage to face whatever it is you have to face. To do this, build a form: structure the disciplines you need to support your progress. If the thing you think you want to do is truly an expression of your soul, the form will enable you to find your passion for it. But if what you thought you needed to do is just a fancy of the ego, you will discover that as well. Keep looking for messages from your soul's intentions, and, with time and directed efforts toward what you believe your soul's mission is, your true passion and purpose will reveal themselves.

In any case, the important thing is to build a form. Choose two disciplines that heighten your self-awareness. (My favorites are yoga and meditation, but there are tons of others.) Choose two action steps directly related to what you want to succeed in accomplishing. Maintain integrity with every single one of them—meaning, show up for them with great regularity—and keep at it until you feel a flow of energy passing through the form that is moving your life forward and upward. Don't stop! Keep going until the day comes when you have a specific experience that tells you, beyond a shadow of any doubt, that you have fulfilled your soul's mission and have mastered your life.

LIVING FROM CAUSE

So, there you have it: my story, along with the fundamental methodology for spiritual growth and accelerated soul evolution established by the teachings of Walt Baptiste.

At this point, I feel the need to stop and take a moment to give you something to consider: what does it mean to be human?

I believe that we are nearing a time when the old definitions aren't so valid; in fact, in this day and age, they're flawed. People today need a new vision. It's time to redefine the full meaning of being a human. I don't mean that you have to give up what you already know: to grow up, marry, work hard, and then die. Yes, those are typical markers of a human life. But for me, being human also means to expand, grow, and heighten the state of our being. That is the result of the *work* of Walt's methodology. Embracing the soul and spiritual nature of *ourselves* and the spiritual nature of Life *while* meeting life's material responsibilities develops the *whole human.*

I believe we are at a turning point in human history. We as humans are passing through a period of explosive evolution. Humanity is leaving behind the usual human condition of living from the past, responding to life only from the effects of what our personal history tells us about who we are and what we believe to be true about life.

People who normally respond from the effects of their past while being driven by the ego of their unsubstantiated beliefs—and who couple that with rarely giving deep consideration to their true nature or their futures— discover they cannot find lasting happiness. That life path is not enough for many of the souls who are here today. They seek deeper meaning and worth in their lives. These people persistently ask, "What is my latent potential? What is my genius and my inspiration, and how can I use it to contribute in a meaningful way?" They thrive on change. They seek the energy highs that accompany inspired ideas. They know there is more to life than what they are experiencing now, and they're determined to find what's missing.

What *is* missing? There is no clear, strong, eternal, unchanging foundation based on the truths of nature to which they can declare allegiance and by which they can live. What's missing are the truths of human nature, or the nature of Life Itself that their *own intuitive instincts tell them, have been, and always will be forever, real.*

But I know this to be true: by living from *Cause (Soul)* and through a "living process," you will free yourself from the negative, small-minded prison of your past while blossoming beautifully into the love, the intelligence, the full, whole embodiment of your highest potential.

In Part II of this book, we'll get down to the detailed work of doing the best you can to uncover your soul's unique *good*-ness (that goodness that's alive and well in the core center of every individual, waiting to be expressed into life). As a person creating from your unique core, you will carry a little different feel, bring a little different sound to life—a little different mindset that enriches your experience as well as the experiences of your loved ones.

Your unique expression as an individual will bring out your true value to the world around you. The flow of inner purification generated by the combined principles set forth by Walt Baptiste will bring to the surface those higher energies, the higher human character residing secretly at the core of yourself. Discovering them in your life not only benefits you as an individual but is also a critical step on the path back to your True Spiritual Home.

Walt Baptiste used the analogy of a canoe riding the current of a stream back to the ocean. When the person paddling is a beginner, the canoe can easily become snagged in the weeds, or slammed against a fallen tree, or damaged by a hidden rock. A beginner navigator may even lose control finding him or herself riding the current backward—a far cry from the goal, which is to align the canoe at the center of the stream's powerful desire to return home once again to its origin: oceanic waters. Alignment with the stream's desire makes passage near effortless. The same holds true when embracing the flow of the energies of inner purification and spiritual growth created by the structure of the disciplines. No longer are you a sleeping giant. You ride the power of your inner desire, your intuitive intelligence, and the giant power of your core energies back to your Spiritual Home, where all is well.

Using the details laid out in Part II, you no longer have to be a beginner. In fact, there is a good possibility you are already participating in the stream of life in ways you hadn't realized. This will provide you with a complete vision. In fact, my reason for the book is to put it all there with clarity, holding nothing back. If you are ready, if you are aflame with desire, then with the guru's methodology, you can easily tread the Path of the Masters back to your True Spiritual Home: it's simply a matter of making that conscious choice to *willingly step into* the thrill of the adventure.

Part II
The True Art of Life

3

Writing for Realization

When the village puts its head to pillow at night for sleep, he who grew the most that day is happiest.

—*AUTHOR UNKNOWN*

All of us must serve materiality for the privilege of being a part of this world. But it seems we are happiest when serving the soul's need even as we fulfill the responsibilities that materiality demands of us. And we become even happier by expanding our conscious recognition of Spirit within ourselves *and* outside ourselves throughout life.

To serve the soul's needs and to refine the senses required to experience Spirit, you have to make an effort through right actions, driven by desire and passion: the passion to know your soul's desire for this lifetime, or the desire to have spiritual experiences. Right action comes in many forms, but at the top of the list is meditation, accompanied by yoga or another discipline that heightens self-awareness, such as tai chi, martial arts, or any creative art form: dance, playing a musical instrument, painting, or pottery (along with yoga, cooking works for me). Whatever your chosen discipline for developing greater self-awareness, it must be something you are extremely passionate—*there's that word again*—about perfecting. This is a must in order to engage the process of ongoing improvement toward the goal of self-mastery.

With your burning desire and sincere right action, you are asking for the "call" from Spirit—a call that ignites the heart even more. Your life takes on a new direction that you will never give up—even if some part of you wanted to, you *couldn't* give it up.

But here's the thing about the call: It comes in its own time. You don't create it. You can't create it, because the nature of the call is an experience (or a series of experiences) that demonstrates the greatest possible outcome for your life. It is an outcome that is *beyond your imagination*. Sometimes the call may be a moment of experiencing the divine nature of yourself that is awe-inspiring *beyond* words. It kindles your passion, and you want *more*! Trusting that the call will come to you is an important component as you proceed with your right action.

As for me, I received two life-changing calls. The first was my initial yoga class with Walt Baptiste, which set my heart ablaze for weeks. I was young and didn't know it would be wise to keep the experience to myself. Instead, I blabbed about it, both privately and publicly, to anyone who would listen. (I learned later that speaking too much about the specifics of a spiritual experience would dilute its impact.) The second call was my experience in the coffee shop described in chapter 1. I had barely clarified what happened that day in my mind when my divorce interrupted my joy. Nevertheless, during my eight "down" years, I never let go of the call. I couldn't use it to help others then; I had to confirm on the deepest levels the power of the principles I'd discovered so that I could heal myself internally of all my limiting beliefs and emotional wounds. Still, the call remained a part of my meditations and journaling.

LET YOUR INSTINCTS GUIDE YOU

Take a moment to be clear about your intentions here. You are asking to expand, to grow into a higher human life experience—not to surrender all that you know on the material level, but rather to expand, to embrace *consciously* the soul nature of yourself as well as the spiritual nature of yourself and of life.

Let your instincts guide you. The ultimate goal of meditation is to realize Spirit ignited by the practice. But do your instincts tell you that seeking union with Spirit is where your passions lie? As I mentioned in chapter 2, many people do not identify with that goal. More often, people start with something of personal importance to them: *Why was I born?* or *What is my soul's deepest desire?* Never stop asking, "Who am I? Why am I here?" until you are aligned inside. *Aligned* means that your heart (your subconscious mind), your conscious mind, and your soul's desire are all in agreement with your actions. A passion for life is the natural outcome of alignment.

Soul communication often comes through a passion, a deep desire to do something. Often, these thoughts of doing something won't let you alone. Some people have the same desires kicking around in the back of their minds for years.

Most people have two main areas of development that their soul wants to experience. The first may be a talent or an art form it wants to master. Sometimes, this takes the form of an ingenious, out-of-the-box interpretation of an everyday environment or situation. An example of this is when Walt Baptiste went into a local gym with the intention of working out for the first time. It was on his thirteenth birthday. The young Walt Baptiste never lifted a weight that day. As he stepped into the dimly lit room, he was shocked by what he found: old, dirty mattresses lying about the floor; a group of men standing by a window, smoking cigars and drinking soda; one patron lying on his back on one of the mattresses, doing what we would call bench presses—except there were no benches then. Walt Baptiste turned and left as fast as he had entered, his head ringing with the thought, *I will build a gym that is as gyms are meant to be.* In the years that followed, he built the bench and the slant bench for bench presses. He assembled the first squat rack, the Roman chair, the leg-press machine, and the pull-down bar. He introduced the idea of healthy eating and vitamin supplements for body building and higher health, and he designed a pattern of synchronized breath with each weight-lifting repetition. In 1949, he won the Mr. America body-building title.

How about you? Do you have an out-of-the-box interpretation of an everyday environment that's ingenious? If so, do you have a vision accompanying it, and are you feeling an inspiration, drive, and passion to fulfill that vision?

The second main desire of the soul is to resolve an aspect of life where there is little energy or understanding. A good example is a person who makes large sums of money but is always behind in paying bills. Even with a promotion and raise in salary, it isn't long before this person is behind in monthly bills once again.

I wish I could tell you what your soul's needs are, but the truth is, I can't. You will have to take up the adventure of uncovering them for yourself, just as I did. After all, it's *your* soul's intention for this life cycle, *your* soul's vision of the highest possible outcome for your life experience.

As I mentioned in chapter 2, the spiritual experience that informed me of my soul's purpose occurred after three years of active searching. Finding that deep knowing of why we're here can be frustrating, and it requires a lot of patience. But this is why we practice regular yoga and meditation, both of which develop the gifts of long-term, never-give-up patience.

The best way I can help you is to take you through a few exercises that were big helps to me as I searched for my "right work," as I like to call it. I have given these exercises to groups of people who have also benefited from the synergistic energy created by the group. Great success resulted, and I hope to have many opportunities to lead groups through the exercises again. But the most success I personally experienced with these exercises happened when I was alone. So I know that sitting quietly in a room by yourself can have very powerful results—by which I mean a huge uptick in the number of synchronistic events that life will deliver to you, all of which will serve your deepest desires brought out by the writings.

But the exercises must be done properly. Wasting time and energy in any endeavor produces the opposite result of the one you are looking for. Every endeavor has its guidelines and principles for success. To ensure success, it's up to you to learn these and take them seriously enough to follow them carefully. Then you will not squander time or energy.

Success in these writing exercises requires that an internal chemistry be created that takes you out of the reasoning mind and into the heart so powerfully that another mind—the mind of internal knowing—becomes engaged as well. The outcome is nothing short of realizing things about your nature and your character that you never realized before. The hoped-for result is a delightful experience that neither the conscious nor the subconscious will easily forget.

Remember, these are soul-searching exercises. They are not meant to elicit reasoned thoughts from the memories of your past, or ego-driven ideas of what you want life to be. Open yourself instead! Be spontaneous with your words. Throw yourself into the writing with abandon. Let your soul reveal its secrets to you.

GUIDELINES FOR THE WRITING EXERCISES

The exercises here are divided into two sections. You will need to dedicate time separately to each one. After completing Section One, "Defining Your Relationship Values," try not to let too much time pass before addressing Section Two, "Addressing Your Life Lesson." You should begin Section Two within seven days after you do Section One.

Section One is designed for you to visit and reestablish your positive relationship values—those you exhibit with the ones you love the most. These values may include things such as expressions of love or nurturing, caring for someone's well-being, kindness, generosity, speaking to loved ones from the heart, and so on. These are character qualities of the soul as well as human character qualities. You will encounter a series of questions to be answered in timed sections of ten minutes each. Hidden within your responses to the timed writings are your relationship values—so a subsequent process is provided for deciphering your timed writings.

There are two reasons for establishing your relationship values. First, if you observe with sincerity the principles laid out in this book, an accelerated energy will move your life forward and upward. The area of your life that will be affected most will be that of your relationships. After visiting your relationship values, you will find a kinder, more loving voice emanating from you in a very natural way—not only toward your family and loved ones but also toward close friends. The changes won't stop there. With time, you'll notice yourself demonstrating high relationship values even with acquaintances. Ultimately, as you become fully integrated, everyone you encounter will receive the benefit of your elevated relationship values. The second reason for establishing your relationship values is simply this: when you give conscious consideration to your positive relationship values, life is a lot more joyful and *a lot easier*!

After the timed exercises, Section One includes three questions to be answered directly. These additional questions begin to address your soul's needs and its desire to express itself.

Section Two attempts to uncover your soul's lesson for this life cycle by visiting your weaknesses. This is a little harder than it sounds. You will have to be brutally honest with yourself and go to places you may not necessarily want to go. But the good news is that no one else is going to read what you write—so you're free to be deeply honest. Still, some people find themselves holding back for no real reason except that they lack the courage to really face a negative hardship that, deep inside, they acknowledge they have created.

Before beginning, please commit to these guidelines:

Demonstrate your respect for the process. Don't schedule a small amount of time thinking that you'll do a little now and more later. Give yourself one hour *each* for Section One and Section Two. It might take you the full two hours to complete both sections, or you might finish in an hour and half; it doesn't matter. (Truthfully, though, if it takes you less than sixty minutes to complete both sections, there is a good chance that you were in your reasoning mind the whole time.) The important thing is to find a time when there are no distractions. Put yourself in a quiet place where life cannot reach you. This is sometimes not as easy as it sounds, but it is an absolute must.

Be firm; be determined. Make the commitment that you will not stop Section One or Section Two until you've given thorough attention to every exercise. One caveat: I have given these exercises to people who became so emotional during the course of them that they couldn't continue. If this happens to you, it's a good idea to stop and wait for another opportunity; then begin again from the beginning.

You will need a clean, 8-1/2" x 11" notebook. Do not use a diary or journal-size notebook. You will need room—space to really let fly your emotions. Anything smaller is too confining.

You will also need a timer.

When you write, do so knowing that no one else is ever going to read what you write. You are doing this for yourself and only yourself, so what ends up on the page is strictly between you and that page.

It is not advisable to do this in close proximity to someone else in your life, such as a spouse. When I give these exercises in person and there are couples in the room, I ask the partners to move out of range of each other. If someone is sitting too close to a loved one, this can cause holding back because one person thinks the other will want to know what he or she wrote. Don't do that to yourself. Create a setting where you can pour yourself into the writings with abandon.

DON'T CHANGE THE RECIPE

Now, here are five specific rule's that will help you navigate the process. Please follow them carefully. Do not change the recipe!

Rule 1:

In Section One, you will find a series of topics or questions. Except for a few specific questions, everything that you write in response *must be in the form of a descriptive story.* (Example: if you're writing about the things you love about your father, it might look like, "I remember when my father came home late from work. He would always check to see if I was sleeping, and if I wasn't, he'd sit on the bed and ask me about my day. He did that *every* night. I loved our time together, so I would try to stay awake as long as I could.") Write about the big things and the littlest details—the tone in someone's voice when he or she speaks to you; how people let you know how much they think about and care about you; how you feel when you are with someone; the little things people do to make you feel loved and valued. But, above all else, write every loving thought that pops into your head in story form. I've watched as people write in list form—even if tempted, do not write a list. Write as though you are speaking your thoughts as a story. There is a reason for every nuance.

Rule 2:

Once you begin writing, just keep your pen moving, no matter what. If you run out of thoughts, then write something like, "Oh, look, I don't know what else to write here. I guess I could…" and so on, until something new comes into your mind, which it will. But until then, keep your pen moving; don't let it stop. People tend to ignore this principle the most, because the ego interferes. When you ignore it, though, you've moved from the heart to the reasoning mind and are thinking from memory. Don't do that to yourself. Write from the heart and let another, deeper mind enter.

Rule 3:

The writings in Section One are timed at ten minutes each, which should fill an 8-1/2" x 11" page. If you fill the page before ten minutes, go on to a new one. If passion and desire are strong and you want to write longer, do so.

Rule 4:

The best outcome of these exercises is a breakthrough of self-discovery. Let that be your intention. That said, give up all thoughts of a successful outcome (e.g., that big *aha* moment when a light turns on and you know your reason for being). Give up, too, all doubt that says this is a waste of time or that it's not going to work. Let me repeat: throw yourself into the work with abandon. The subconscious will respond in amazing ways without you realizing it if you let go of all preconditioning. By writing with wholehearted commitment, you are aligning yourself with the cycles of a life adventure that will prove to you undeniably the reason for your being. But the "oh my God" realization experience has its own timing. Remember, it took me three years of searching before that amazing experience in the coffee shop. So, write with abandon!

If you feel your emotions beginning to engage, you're there—go with it strongly. I've seen many tears from both men and women as they moved their pens across the page.

Rule 5:

Commit to addressing every exercise in both Section One and Section Two in one sitting each. (Though, as I mentioned before, you can take up to a week between the two sections.) Yes, this can seem tedious, and the wrist and fingers can tire. But there are no free rides. Everything has its cost, and anything of worth takes effort. Promise yourself that you are willing to pay the expense by expending your sincere effort.

THE WRITING EXERCISES: SECTION ONE

First, choose either your father or mother—the one to whom you are (or were) closest. If you do not consider yourself close to either parent, it is all right to choose a mother or father *figure*—perhaps an aunt, uncle, or grandparent, or anyone who was a positive, life-affirming influence on you while you were growing up.

Write down all the things that you love(d) about your parent of choice— all the ways they demonstrate(d) love to you or the ways you experienced love from them. If it's your father you're writing about, an example might be. "When my father was home, I always felt comfortably safe around him. He never felt distant or disconnected from me, even when it was clear he was worried about work, which was often. The moment I wanted his attention, he'd put aside his problems and spend real time with me." If it's your mother, an example might be, "When my mother was feeling a lot of stress, she would stop everything and bake sweet goodies for us. By the time she pulled the pie or the cake or cookies from the oven, she was in love again with the most important things in her life: my siblings, my dad, and me. Boy, those sweets were so good."

Remember: write down *in story form* all the things you love(d) about your parent or parent figure. Time your writing for ten minutes without stopping.

Next, select your wife or husband or someone you are (or were) deeply in love with. Following the same instructions that applied to your parent, write down all the things that you love(d) about this person: all the ways they demonstrate(d) love to you. It can be helpful to draw on some of the most loving moments from the past when you really knew this person loved you. It can also be helpful to remember when you first found love with this person and recall all of what you found to be so loving in them then (remembering that we all change).

Write with abandon, immersing yourself to the point where your emotions engage strongly as you write.

Next, select the daughter or son to whom you are closest. If you do not have children, then select a favorite sibling; if you have no sibling, then select your favorite closest relative or lifelong friend—someone you have in mind that you really want to include in this exercise. Follow the instructions from the previous exercises. Watch for the emotions to engage even more and the love for this person to build beyond what you thought you would feel when you began. If and when this happens, let go of the time limit. Keep pouring out your emotions until everything that wants to be expressed is revealed on the page.

When you've finished, lean back a moment to breathe and relax, shaking out the kinks in your fingers, wrist, and arm.

Now, while you are in this open state, pretend that God appears at the foot of your bed, saying He will give you one gift—absolutely anything you want—the *one thing* that will make you the most happy in your life right this minute. What is that gift? Answer spontaneously, without thinking about it. Your answer should be something that truly fills your heart with love when you think about it. For me, it's the opportunity to tell people who I am and to share my life story. When I think about doing this, joy wells up strongly within me.

Next, ask yourself what you are really passionate about doing—in fact, the thing you are *most passionate* about doing—and write it down. Be open to the idea that it may be a desire you've had for many years but until now have pushed to the back of your mind. Try not to catch yourself thinking about the limitations of time, education, money, or distance. Remember: no one except you will read what you write, so exercise your freedom to write your *deepest truth*. There is a good chance that what you write here is what you asked God to give to you. Of course, it's OK if these two answers are not the same; we're just looking for the *deeper, true desires of your heart*.

Now, ask yourself what one positive thing you've always been really, really good at and write it down. If you are too humble to admit that you are really good at something, then pick something that other people have praised you for.

Once more, if you need to, lean back again for a moment to breathe and relax, and shake out the kinks in your fingers, wrists, and arms. Now, please return to the pages of your first series of writings.

MAKING SENSE OF SECTION ONE

At the top of a clean page, write the words, "I value."

Go through your writings and assign a word or two to every action or characteristic you love about your loved ones. For example, you may have written, "I love the way my father opened my bedroom door every night to check on me before he went to bed. Sometimes he would whisper something, telling me how much he loved me, or how beautiful he thought I was." Your value words might be, *sweet, loving attention*. Or you may have written, "I knew when my mother was irritated about something or someone, because I could see the tension she was holding by the frown lines on her face. But the moment I asked her for something, all her tension disappeared as she responded wholeheartedly with a loving smile." Your value words might be, *spontaneous, selfless love*.

On your page marked "I value," write in list form *all* the key words you find that represent the *essence* of the loving experiences you shared together or the things you love about your loved ones. Next, select from the list and eliminate duplications and similarities. Now, select the seven value words that are the *most important* to you and mark them. Then, number the most important seven values in the order of their importance to you. On a clean sheet of paper, write your seven most important key words. These are your most important values in any relationship. Feel free to list more.

What you love *about* the ones you love is alive and well in yourself and is part of who you are. Look closely at your seven most important relationship values. They are *your* values, because if they didn't exist inside you—if they weren't a part of you—you wouldn't have noticed them being expressed by your loved ones. If you were to create a list along with a sibling who grew up in the same household as you, the lists the two of you created would be different simply because your sibling wouldn't have noticed the same things you did. What is a part of them is not necessarily a part of you.

What you requested from God and the thing you are passionate about doing could represent your soul's need at present. This needs to be considered.

The thing you have always been good at may be a talent wanting to express itself. Again, this is worth considering.

The writings you have just produced in Section One of these exercises were meant to provide possible new insights into who you are and what your higher life values are. The exercises were also crafted to expose an important soul need in your life. Maybe you gained some insights, but perhaps you have not yet. Maybe you have become really clear about your soul's needs and talent. If you have, congratulations. But if you are still confused or not feeling confident about your soul and its needs, don't worry. Keep asking; the answers will show up. And when they do, they will be authentic. You will know this to the nth degree, and no one will be able to convince you otherwise.

THE WRITING EXERCISES: SECTION TWO

Next, let's look more closely at your soul's lesson. This section is not actually timed, although, again, you should allow one hour to complete it.

As I mentioned earlier, the soul has two areas that are its main concerns: one is a talent it wants to master; the other is a challenge of this life, an aspect of yourself that you have a great need to develop, learn about, and finally, refine—also to the point of mastery. It would be nice if we were all here only to display to the world some amazing talent. But, alas, most of us are also here to face a very real challenge within a particular area of life or with regard to a particular character trait.

A life lesson can be needed in an area where there is little conscious understanding of what's required and very little will to correct the problem. I'll give you an example: my own life lesson. I was out of sync with the demands of family life. There came the day when I was sick and tired of feeling that I couldn't live up to what was required to be a good husband and a father to three boys. I had ignored this problem for far too long. Out of my frustration, I sat down, intending to face the problem head on and with brutal honesty. As I give you the instructions for this exercise, I'll let you know what I did to address my problem and the experiences I had as a result.

First, think about the areas in your life that you believe need attention. When I first did these exercises, I broke my life into its three most troubled categories at the time: husband, father, and career. However, your categories can be from any part of your life: spirituality, health, money, relationships, career, marriage, parenting, fitness, and so on. The only criterion is that you consider your *most* troubling categories. Try not to choose more than four.

Initially, choose the one "sick-and-tired" area where you feel the greatest pain. Then list all the ways you are sick and tired of acting negatively or not participating as you should. Then do the same with the remaining categories. I experienced my greatest pain as a father, so I listed all the ways I was sick and tired of my actions as a father to three beautiful boys.

Here are a few examples of what I wrote down. I was sick and tired of:

- Not really knowing what a good father actually is
- Not following through with my promises to my children
- Demonstrating a low integrity level toward them as if they weren't a high priority for me
- *Not really knowing* who my children were
- Feeling irritated when asked to do something for them

Then I made a long list of all the ways I was sick and tired of the way I acted as a husband toward my wife. It's important to note that I did not use the list to complain about my wife's problems and how I wanted her to change. No! I focused on my deficiencies as a husband and how I needed to step up to be a better one.

I wasn't so successful with the career category. First, I wrote that I was sick and tired of not finding my "right work." Right then, I froze. My mind was blank for the longest time, and finally, out of desperation, I simply wrote, "I want to earn my living out of who I am." I was sick and tired of not doing so.

Once you have your lists of "sick and tireds," begin again with a clean page. Go through your list of "sick and tireds" and write sentences that reverse and resolve each painful sentence. For example:

- In my category of parenting, I had written that I was sick and tired "of not really knowing what a good father actually is." Afterward, I wrote, "I won't stop until I know everything there is to know about being a good father, and then I *will* put what I've learned into action."
- To address the needs of the second sentence—of not following through with my promises to my children—I wrote, "When I make a promise to my children, I *will keep it every time!*"
- On demonstrating a low integrity level toward my children, I wrote, "Whenever I am around my children, I *will* remain *present* to the point of being in harmony with their *joy, their* needs!"
- Concerning *not really knowing* who my children were, I wrote, "I *will* never stop relating to each child individually until I *clearly, clearly* know all that I can know about who they are as individuals—their strengths, their struggles, their beauty."
- As for being irritated when asked to do something for them, I wrote, "I *will never again* feel irritation and instead feel only joy because I've been asked to do something for them!"

Regarding this final point, it is helpful to remember that your declarative sentences state *ideals* that you are passionate about taking up. Did I still feel irritated when a child demanded my attention? Yes—and, in fact, often at first. But I no longer let them knew I was irritated. As time passed, I moved closer to the ideal response. My irritation gave way to the honor I felt at being able to serve them. My new levels of engagement in their lives brought me great joy and happiness. I especially loved learning their natures as individuals, which surfaced more and more as the quality of our time together grew.

After I wrote my declarations, I went on to write statements of considerate actions that I planned to undertake in order to reverse my inefficiencies as a husband. In truth, once I started writing the reversing sentences in this category, the words simply poured onto the page. I couldn't help it. The tears began to flow as well. The faster I wrote, the faster my tears flowed. I was beyond the reasoning mind, beyond the ego; I had in fact reached deeply into my state of being that understood the essence of my problems. With that, a powerful energy was born to resolve my pain in every area of my life.

Notice that each example of a resolving sentence emphasizes the word *will*. Try to use the word *will* in your sentence each time. Use it to feel your greatest desire to resolve the situation. I wrote one sentence for each situation because I felt such a rush of strong desire with each one. That was me. But you might write more than one sentence. In fact, you may have a lot to say about your new attitudes and actions for each resolution sentence. Go with it.

AFTER THE WRITING EXERCISES

When you, with deep, sincere passion, complete the writing exercises, Real Life will respond for as long as you take action to find the answer to or fulfill the reason that you were born, or to discover what your area of unique contribution to life might be, or work daily to resolve the "sick and tireds" you've resolved to address.

Through the writings in both sections, you are looking for that time when you can no longer ignore your soul's deeper intentions for this life and you are overcome with a passion to *do something about them*. Reading through your answers to the three questions in Section One (what you requested from God, what you are passionate about, what you are really good at) and your list of "sick and tireds," choose one area that instills in you the greatest desire, the greatest passion to fulfill or resolve.

You may have had a huge *aha* moment when you were given the gift of realizing the talent your soul has the desire to bring to the world while mastering its service to others. If that is the area of your strongest passion, focus on making life choices that serve your vision. Or perhaps you are feeling a great level of disappointment because you didn't uncover your soul's genius. Turn your attention solely to finding the answer to the question of why you were born. Or maybe your greatest concern is resolving one of your life issues that has been a real problem for far too long. If that is the case, look thoughtfully at your sentences of resolving ideals. Choose the *one* action you are most interested in reversing and focus your conscious action choices on resolving your soul's life lesson. For example, in my list of parenting "sick and tireds," I chose to focus all my attention on resolving my habit of communicating irritation when asked to do something for one of my children. As our relationship improved through my right efforts, my understanding of who my children really are also improved. In fact, all my "sick and tired" complaints were greatly improved by the process, because, as they say, a rising tide raises all boats.

When you successfully live the new life experiences of a resolved "sick and tired" or the mastery of your genius's talent, you will have become a different person—different in an expanded way. Because you are different, you'll have different life experiences. Take a few moments to consider the new life experiences you would enjoy: the joys of success you'd like to live because of your courage. Make a list of those desired experiences. Read your list every day. Decide on the time of the day you will read your list, and never fail to read it then. (The best times are before sleep or upon waking, when the subconscious is most open to suggestion.) Try to indulge your mind with the images and feelings of your favorite experience. When you're finished, go about your day and give up all attachment to expectations about outcomes from your list.

The next key to succeeding is to remain focused—in terms of body, mind, and daily actions—on what is needed for forward movement. At the same time, be open to that part of your inner subconscious mind that acts as your guide. Stay fluid and flexible and responsive to new directions.

The outcome of this natural process is the inner recognition of a steady, refining development of the higher human elements within yourself: human traits like intuition, positive intentions of being good and doing good, compassion, joy, love, insights, instincts, wisdom, greater connection with loved ones, and increasing moments of being in a state of grace. At the same time, life gradually becomes less adversarial, more harmonious. All of these are indicators of an individual who lives from his or her soul's nature, guided by his or her Higher Mind.

After I undertook these writings, it wasn't long before all the wonderful guiding signs in my life accelerated dramatically. I was repeatedly presented with events that seemed to be orchestrated specifically for the purpose of resolving my shortcomings as a father and husband. Even overheard conversations or words coming from a radio or TV speaker clearly addressed my life on a very personal level. The unfolding of these events represented the real "life behind life," as I like to call it.

When it comes to discovering the life behind life, meditation is a huge help. Meditation at the third-eye level heightens and refines one's sensitivity to the intuitive impulse. This is useful, since it is your intuition that senses which event (or events throughout the day) have been orchestrated for your inner purification or edification.

I want to be really clear here: when your evolution accelerates, personal, divinely orchestrated events happen *every day*! Intuition not only senses those outside events but also senses more clearly the thoughts entering the mind that are, in fact, coming from the Higher Mind that Walt Baptiste spoke about—i.e., the Mind that's higher than the reasoning mind. Meditation refines the intuitive sense that catches those higher thoughts and imbues a rich depth of understanding surrounding the knowledge they contain. The intuitive impulse is also of great help when witnessing the life outside of you (like relevant snippets of conversation) that also communicates something meant for you on a personal level—the meaning behind the meaning of what you have just witnessed or experienced.

One example is the time I quit a perfectly good job selling furniture to work for a retailer that sold appliances. I switched jobs because the new manager promised a hassle-free increase in income. The moment I started working at my new job, though, I doubted my decision. Something wasn't right. The first customer I helped was a nervous wreck. She kept asking question after question—seemingly silly, obvious questions—rapid fire, one on top of the other, without even waiting for the answers to the first questions. Her husband, standing behind her, rolled his eyes. No sooner had they left when the next customer *did the same thing*! Likewise, the third customer. I was in the wrong place, and my intuitive responses to the anxious customers were mirroring a high level of anxiety within myself. It was clear to me that there was a wiser sense in my Self that understood the mistake I had made by switching. The next day, I went back to the manager of the furniture store. Before I could say a word, he said, "I wondered when you would come to your senses"—interesting wording!—and welcomed me back.

When your evolution accelerates, you will encounter *a lot of these kinds of experiences*. And a heightened intuitive sensitivity doesn't miss them. Thank God for the gifts of meditation.

Before we move on, it's important to understand that the writing exercises are not meant to be experienced once and then forgotten. You really should revisit them once a year. January or February are always a good time, since it is natural to begin a new year with a well-defined desire for your healings and learning experiences for the coming twelve cycles of personal evolution (more on this in the following chapter). But, then again, any time you're inspired to go through the writing exercises is the right time.

As for me, I usually like to review my relationship values near the end of January and see what I learned the year before. I review my successes and note who I have become as a result of the past year's adventure. Just how much did I mature, strengthen, and evolve—and in what aspects of my character? All of this gives me a feeling for what I'd like to experience during the upcoming year. Then, in February, I watch for the "call" that provides the vision for the coming year's adventure, which is always *bigger and more inspiring* than what my everyday mind could have imagined (more about this in the next chapter as well).

We are all creators—creating our every moment, whether awake or asleep. We create as the universe creates. The universe is in a constant state of creating itself in a fluid movement, moving in three basic directions. It's creating anew, sustaining what has been created, or contracting and breaking down. Deep, personal soul intention creates in the same fluid way via the nature of life. The experiences that expand and elevate your meaning in life are created in fluid life cycles, and these forces of movement create the path to your successful outcome. This movement alternates between contracting, or breaking down, how you experience life, and expanding who you are into someone greater than before.

If we think about it, nature moves in reliable cycles: four seasons to a year; twenty-four hours to a day; twelve months to a year; new, flowering growth in the spring; crop harvesting in the fall, and so on. The principles of psychological maturity and soul evolution also move in reliable cycles. In the following chapter, we'll examine those cycles in great, clear detail and see how they affect us internally: how they are the cause of our maturity, of our soul's evolution.

4

Those Strange Cycles

When I think back, it's hard to believe that during the first twelve months the Hungry Mouth Restaurant was open, we worked an average of one hundred hours a week, seven days a week, with no scheduled breaks. Our only day off that year was Christmas Day. About four months into that year, when I was silently doubting just how long I would be able to keep up the pace, Walt Baptiste came into the kitchen where we all gathered after closing. "Can any of you tell me," he began, his tone deliberate, "where, in any book, or during any speech, or in any movie, or anywhere, for that matter, where it has been said"…he paused…"that working for a spiritual master was going to be easy?"

It's amazing how one well-timed question coming from a spiritual master can change everything. My inner response was, *Now I understand. This is a test of character strength.* And that was fine with me. It was one of the reasons I was there: to grow up by strengthening my character as a man. But Walt's question opened a new possibility. To me, this work was a challenge. It was not a challenge of the ego, of the "watch me win" nature, but rather, it made me ask myself, "How much will I learn here by stepping well beyond my limitations every day?" Also, by this time, I had become aware that an environment created by a spiritual master is like no other. The energies in the restaurant were charged with Walt Baptiste's intentions. I wanted to know what would happen to me, to my life, if I stayed there, no matter the level of difficulty.

Of course, during the following years, I had many learning experiences on many levels. One of the most interesting was my newfound sense of life's cycles. With all those consecutive hours working in a charged environment as a chef, which is a creative art form—all day long, week after week, month after month, year after year—I began to sense certain cycles of experiences repeating over and over each year.

In the beginning months of a year, a lot of questions about the direction of my life, as well as about my goals and desires, would naturally run through my mind. During the early spring months, I experienced a lot of internal back and forth: various competing desires within myself, perhaps wanting to leave and do something else. Real questions about myself as well as my work as a chef kept popping up, and I wanted answers. As the months progressed into summer, all of that would be forgotten, for the most part. Instead, what followed was a long period of intense work, through August and often into the first days of September. As the end of August approached, the intensity of my work always increased dramatically. This was followed by a time of great discovery somewhere in early September. The answers to all my questions and concerns, *and more*, came to me either through various experiences or simply by information flooding into my mind, or both. October and November presented a combination of intense work and more experiences of informed learning's. In December, everything seemed to smooth out. Life was more fun. A kind of "new me" emerged: I had new levels of energy accompanied by new levels of self-confidence.

JOSEPH CAMPBELL AND THE HERO'S JOURNEY

I had no idea what these repeating rhythms were about. I assumed they were a part of being an adult and that everyone experienced them. When I tried to talk about these rhythms with other people, they had no idea what I was referring to. It turned out they were unaware of any such cycles. So I had to remain content with witnessing them on my own—until the day I discovered Joseph Campbell.

Campbell is known for his knowledge of and insights into the myths of the world, a subject that fascinated him from an early age. His own quest began with a single question: "How could it be that a simple story might bore listeners, while a myth is able to captivate listeners' attention for hours?" His question remained unanswered for years until, in 1929, the first year of the Great Depression, he decided to move into an isolated cabin in Woodstock, New York. His goal was to study every myth he could lay his hands on so he could find the secret of their power to captivate.

When Joseph Campbell emerged from the wilderness five years later, he offered the world his seminal book, *The Hero's Journey*. He wrote that all heroic myths found anywhere in the world throughout recorded history had the same structure, or storytelling conditions. He named and defined twelve conditions: the Ordinary World; the Call to Adventure; the Reluctant Hero; the Wise Old Man or Woman; Into the Underworld; Tests, Allies, and Enemies; the Innermost Cave; the Supreme Ordeal; Grasping the Sword; the Road Back; Resurrection; and Return to the Ordinary World.

As I read the names and descriptions of these conditions, I was struck with the realization, "Oh my God, these are the cycles I experienced at the stove!" This discovery was incredibly inspiring. In fact, I see now that this was the first piece of the puzzle that preceded the spiritual experience I had had in the café.

Simply defining the twelve conditions is not enough to help you grasp the significance of the cycles of life. I want to be really specific about each condition and how each one affects us internally. To do that, I'll describe the experiences I had in a single year of my life, 1976, and will show how each month fulfilled the conditions of the hero's journey. (I don't mean to suggest that your cycles will, or should, always align with the months in precisely this way, but this is my experience, and I hope that by offering it, I will make you more attentive to the ebb and flow of your own.)

A YEAR IN THE LIFE

January: the Ordinary World

In the month of January 1976, I had been working full time at the Hungry Mouth for a little more than four years. I was "dialed in" to the requirements of the work as well as to Walt Baptiste's teachings. That part was fine. Nevertheless, I was having trouble. I wasn't growing steadily. There was still too much of my old self that stubbornly held to the old beliefs of who I was in the world. I clung to the old, programmed, self-doubting me, lacking in strength of confidence and belief in my own inner wisdom. In that respect, I was stuck. Embedded in my need to realize my inner strength of will and wisdom were seeds of things to come: the conditions for the year's adventure had been established.

February: the Call to Adventure

In February, Walt Baptiste asked me to help him with the building and opening of his new spiritual retreat in El Salvador. It was a clear call to adventure that brought joy to my heart. Honestly, to live in the tropics while serving my guru was a dream come true. It was a dream I had never realized just how much I desired—until I found myself dancing around the kitchen when no one was looking.

March: the Reluctant Hero

In March, Walt Baptiste told me I would be riding along with another student in his truck through Mexico and Guatemala to El Salvador. The truck would be loaded with the tools needed for building tables, chairs, and so on. The idea of driving through Central America scared the wits out of me. My fear got to the point where I stopped saving money for the trip, I put off getting the required medical shots, and I procrastinated when it came to filing for a visa to enter the country.

April: the Wise Old Man or Woman

My fear and self-sabotaging actions endured well into April, until one day, Walt went down the list of requirements for the trip, asking if I had completed them. His exasperation was obvious. "You need to do this," he said firmly. "You need a time of absolute devotion! I want you to commit to staying in El Salvador for one year!" As I heard his words, fear shot straight through me. Fear didn't stop me, though. Without hesitation, I promised I'd stay for one year. "Now," Walt added, "Write a letter telling me why you want to go to El Salvador."

It took more than a week for me to put the letter together. Each attempt brought out new passion, new desires for going. I was reminded of the many parts of myself that I knew would flourish, and by the time the letter was complete, it was clear there that was no way was I going to miss this important opportunity.

May: Into the Underworld

Moving into the "underworld" represents that time when you stop fiddling around with what you know needs to be done. Something happens inside yourself to deepen your commitment to proceed. *Deepening* isn't exactly the word, though; it's more of a wholehearted, "nothing will keep me from accomplishing what I have to do to succeed" kind of determination.

Walt Baptiste (the wise old man) had asked me to write a letter to him at the end of April. I handed him the letter on the seventh day in May— the into-the-underworld month.

As we drove away a week later from the Arguello Boulevard Center, our truck loaded to near overflowing, I remember having that feeling of entering an adventure: seeing the goal, the object of the trip, but having no idea what we would encounter on the way or find once we arrived at our destination.

June: Tests, Allies, and Enemies

At the end of May and into the first week of June, we encountered many tests along our travels through Mexico and Guatemala, but the more intense tests began once we arrived at the guru's newly constructed, beautiful oceanside tropical retreat. Walt Baptiste was there to greet us but had to return to San Francisco in a few days' time. He gave each of us instructions for the work he wanted completed before his return in two or three weeks. We were to keep the plants watered, feed the animals, and build chairs and tables for the large dining room. It was more than enough to keep us busy.

At this point, the overt test was to stay on the property and keep busy with the work. As always, though, the deeper test challenged the "inner enemy." I had to resist the temptation to neglect my responsibilities, leave the premises, and go play. On an even deeper level, I harbored a powerful desire to run away from this strange land—where the food was unfamiliar and no one spoke English. And on a deeper level still, I wanted to run away from the responsibility I was being asked to accept. I wanted to flee, returning to the familiar place I called home. Yes, I wanted to go *home* desperately!

July: the Innermost Cave

Tensions were building. On the first of July, my traveling companion and partner in this adventure threw his belongings into his truck, announcing, "I'm going back to California." As he slid into the driver's seat, he asked if I was coming. My answer was no, but I was filled with contradiction. As I stood on the dirt road, watching the tail end of his truck grow smaller and smaller, my confusion gave way to deep fear. I was now alone in a strange world. But at the same time, something happened in that moment of my decision to remain. Something had risen up within me, and I found I was more resolute than ever about completing my commitment to Walt Baptiste. I would stay there not one day less than a year.

A few days later, Walt and his wife, Magana, returned. For the remaining weeks of July, they gave me an intensive crash course in every aspect of running the retreat: housekeeping, finances, food preparation (very different here than when working in a modern kitchen), buying supplies, taking care of the animals, and so on.

Every day was a wake-up day: I was waking up to the immensity of my responsibility. During these weeks, I was truly a man divided: one part of me fearfully doubted I could ever pull this off without creating some huge catastrophe; a higher part kept repeating, "Pay attention and accept the responsibility. You need to grow up."

August: the Supreme Ordeal

All the mythic conditions are interesting, but to me, the most fascinating is the Supreme Ordeal. In the Innermost Cave, whatever we are working through for the year intensifies. For me, it was the inability to grow in the belief in myself and in the voice of my own inner wisdom. The tests demand our attention and are no longer subtle. We are made to pay more attention and to respond to what we normally would ignore.

In the Supreme Ordeal, intense inner tension ramps up even more, This is followed by an increased desire to hold on to everything representing the old self. The tension becomes so severe that there is a point, near the end of the ordeal, where we simply cannot hold it any longer, and we let go. In that moment of letting go, or shortly thereafter, something amazing happens. Out of nowhere, something shows up, either outside or inside of ourselves, that we never before would have thought of on our own, or something is revealed that offers the perfect solution. Through it all, we are transformed internally. In fact, if we are paying attention and determined to continue, we will never be the same again.

In the last few days of July, two of the guru's other students arrived. In the first week of August, Walt and Magana called a cab and headed to the airport. Before leaving, Walt told me that I was to take care of his students the same way I would take care of visiting strangers. He also gave me money, saying the amount would be more than enough to run everything until his next return. "Let's see how well you can do," was his final comment.

So, here I was, in charge of *his* retreat, *his* buildings, *his* animals, *his* swimming pool, and most important, *his* cherished students. Once again, I watched the tail end of a vehicle grow smaller and smaller as the cab pulled away, but this time, I felt prepared and somewhat confident that I could handle all that might be required.

Two days later, *three more people showed up*! They were Americans who, while traveling in Guatemala, had heard about a spiritual master's retreat in El Salvador and wanted to know if they could stay a week or more. "Ah, yeah, sure," I answered, responding internally once again with both fear and a confident "I can do it" feeling. And I did do it—the best I could, anyway. At least, the guests *seemed* to enjoy themselves.

Near the end of August, everyone had left, and I was feeling uneasy: not because I was alone—I was comfortable with that—but uneasy about the money that remained. The three Americans had paid for their stay, but what I had spent on food to keep everyone satisfied with three meals a day was far more than that. Truthfully, I had overspent in trying to make everything perfect. As I counted the remaining money, adding up what I thought I'd need to get through (food for myself and the animals, paying the property's guardian, and so on), it was clear that I would run out before the guru's return. And when was he returning? I thought it would be in about ten days, but normally I received a letter telling me of his arrival date. I hadn't received anything. Something felt wrong.

At that time, there was no phone service on the property or at any of the homes along our sparsely populated, ocean-view dirt road. To make a call, you had to take a bus to the nearest town with a call center. Once there, you put your name on a list and waited, sometimes hours, for an available phone on which to place an amazingly expensive collect call to America. Nevertheless, I managed to do all this one day, and, back in San Francisco, Norman Wong (Walt Baptiste's most senior student, who had started with his guru in 1956) picked up the phone.

When I asked to speak with Walt, Norman responded, "He's not here. He and Magana are in India. They left a couple of days ago. They'll be back in a month, maybe more." *India?*

Shock and disbelief were not my only responses. Anger was my biggest one, and I let Norman have an earful, finishing with, "What am I supposed to do?" Norman was very gracious. Calmly, he said he didn't know what I could do, but he suggested that maybe he could take up a collection from some of the students and send it to me. I said, "Never mind!" and hung up.

For two days, I was the embodiment of fear and rage. On the third day, I got practical. I surveyed the food supply, considered how to best take care of the animals, and computed how much money (precious little!) would be left after just two weeks when the food would run out. For a few days more, I tried to go on while staying calm and hoping something would happen—perhaps a miracle. But the tension inside of me was growing. I had to work hard to keep from panicking.

One afternoon when I was feeling a lot of anxiety, I lay in a hammock, thinking, *I've got to calm down.* It took some time and a lot of repeating mantra, but ultimately, I settled just enough for a commonsense thought to creep in: *There simply has to be an answer to this.* Suddenly, I was aware that this was a test to see how I would rise to the occasion, and I was *going* to find the solution! I went to the meditation room, promising myself that I wasn't going to move from a seated posture until I had the answer, no matter how long it took.

Needless to say, the first hour of meditation amounted to me listening to a mind out of control, but I settled down as I focused more on mantra. As my mind quieted, I focused on staying open to an answer for why I was in this predicament, what lesson I was to learn, and what the solution was. Whenever more layers of seemingly uncontrollable mind chatter flared up, I returned to my mantra. This back and forth went on for well over an hour. But, as I tired, my most anxious thoughts tired as well. At some point, I let go at a level where I wasn't even attempting to focus or to repeat a mantra. In that near-subconscious void, realizations began to quietly creep in.

The first one was: did I really believe that Walt Baptiste had gone to India, forgetting that I was here? No. Did I really think he didn't know I was alone and would run out of money? Of course he knew. He was a master at orchestrating experiences for his students. Did I really think this was any different from any other test? In my heart, I had always known that Walt would never put anyone in a situation that he or she couldn't find a way out of—so I *must* know the answer.

My realization, in the form of knowing something that was absolutely true, was an experience that engaged all of me. So, for a time, I just enjoyed the aliveness of the feeling and the truth of knowing that the answer I sought was somewhere inside myself. It wasn't long before I couldn't hold that experience any longer either, and I drifted off again into near sub consciousness, for how long I couldn't say. Next, I began to hear clearly these words in my own inner voice: "You know the answer. It's really obvious. It's so obvious, you haven't bothered to recognize it. I'll bet the answer is right in front of you. In fact, I bet the answer is right in front of your face *right now.*" With that, I opened my eyes.

Before I tell you what I discovered, I should explain that at that point in time, the meditation room wasn't really a meditation room. It was planned as our meditation room of the future, although we used it for meditating anyway. In actuality, it was more of a storage room for valuable items that Walt didn't want to lose track of. So when I opened my eyes, the first thing I saw was an empty, plastic five-gallon water bottle, the kind used to stock office water coolers in America. In El Salvador, these bottles were very expensive, so the water company charged a deposit of $25 in Salvadorian money for each one. As the value of what I was looking at—a bottle redeemable for $25—became apparent to me, and as I began looking around the room, I was overcome with laughter—deep, belly-wrenching laughter. Those bottles were *everywhere*!

September: Grasping the Sword

The Supreme Ordeal is followed by Grasping the Sword, which is that part of the cycle in which the adventurer has developed by 51 percent or more into the higher character he or she will embody upon the Return to the Ordinary World (the final phase of a full cycle). The hero has grasped the meaning of the journey and knows how he or she is growing in character because the hero feels it, walks it, and talks it—at least on occasion.

The completion of the journey requires as complete a transformation as possible, so yet more tests are bound to present themselves. For me, now September brought new levels of trust in the spirit within myself as well as greater personal confidence (both were goals of my quest.) I had had the experience of a guiding voice and of knowing that I was connected to it. I was not alone; I was never alone! I knew now more than ever that any answer to any challenge I had to face was inside of me. And since I had achieved this revelation through direct experience, no one could ever take it away from me or convince me it wasn't real.

On a practical level, I *knew* that whatever money the bottle deposits totaled would be enough to keep the retreat center healthy and would last, with perfect timing, until Walt's return. All I had to do was keep a close eye on expenses.

October: the Road Back (More Tests)

September gave way to October. In the second week, I received a letter from Gurudev saying he would be returning in a month. He would be staying for several weeks to get the retreat in shape for a group of guests who would arrive toward the end of November.

Before leaving those many months ago, Walt had asked me to please drain the swimming pool once any visitors left. Running the filters every day was very expensive, and it was needless when no one was there. In his latest letter, he asked me to refill the pool and reminded me that the water had to be crystal clear. "I need to see the bottom of the pool so clearly that I can't see the water in the pool."

It takes more than a week to fill a pool of that size with a garden hose, so once the water reached the halfway mark, I wanted to get the filter started. All went well until I realized that the filtering pump was running but not pumping water. I was not at all familiar with pool-filtering systems, but our property's guardian had a little experience. "We have to prime the pump," he said with an air of authority. Nice try, but that didn't work despite many attempts. In fact, nothing worked. And the more it didn't work, the more reactive I became. *I couldn't let Walt Baptiste down!*

Finally, after more than a week of frustration, I took the bus to the nearest town and asked around. "Does anyone know about pool repair?" Yes, I was told, go see José at this address. After some cajoling, José agreed to meet me the next day—which turned into three days. In the end, it turned out he knew little more than the guardian! Now what?

November: Resurrection

Resurrection is another interesting condition. It's the final test to see how you handle yourself. Here lie final challenges of the year's adventure: some of them are not so demanding, but others are even more intense than the Supreme Ordeal.

The pump-filter problem continued into November. Two weeks before the guru's return, I finally got lucky, finding the address of a pool-supply and repair store in the capital city of San Salvador. Taking public transportation to get there was pretty much a full-day project, but I didn't care. Nevertheless, frustration after frustration continued as I was promised an "expert" repairman in a day or two, maybe three, who never showed. Three trips to the city, three times he didn't come. Unfortunately, someone else did come.

In the midst of all this, a gentleman accompanied by six militarily clad companions, complete with rifles and side arms, showed up at our gate. The leader said he was there to ask my permission to enter the property and inspect the wood products we might have. Some types of wood were considered illegal if cut from protected trees, and he believed we had some of that illegal wood on the grounds. I told him he was asking the wrong person for permission, since I wasn't the property owner. I explained I was there to look after the center until the owner returned, which would be in seven days.

The man's eyes narrowed as he asked, "Are you *sure* you won't let me onto the property?"

Yes, I was sure. If he wanted permission, I told him, come back in seven days. "I'm sure Walt Baptiste will show you around. I don't have the authority."

Two days later, another man showed up at the front gate (like the first, he had a military backup ensemble). I signed for the official-looking document he handed me. As the man left, the guardian, who had witnessed both encounters, looked at me with one of those Cheshire-cat smiles. He had placed his wrists together, implying I would be placed in handcuffs and sent to prison. Sure enough, the paper in my hand was a summons. I had to appear in front of an official of the Department of Interior in seven days.

The first day of Walt's return was not fun. Although he did enjoy the water-bottle story, he was not at all pleased with the condition of the pool. And while he appreciated the protective attitude I had shown toward the property, he said I should have gone ahead and let the government official look around. It wouldn't have hurt anything.

The next day, Walt drove early to the city and talked with the owner of the pool store, after which the pool repairman showed up *that afternoon*! I should have asked Walt what he had said to that man.

When the day came for my "appointment" with the Interior official in San Salvador, Walt drove me there. The official asked for an explanation. As I talked, he interrupted with questions: Why was I there in the first place? What were my responsibilities? How much was I paid? After being satisfied that he had the whole picture, he said, "It's clear you are working at Mr. Baptiste's property without a job permit from our government, which we wouldn't have issued you, because we want those jobs to go to Salvadorians. You have three days to leave the country." He stamped my passport and inserted a paper that I was to give to customs officials the day I left. As I turned to leave, passport in hand, he said, "And, Mr. Walter, next time one of our officials asks to step onto your property—let them."

In the car, Walt asked how it had gone. Honestly, it was hard to tell him. I tried to soften the news by saying I had to leave the country, but maybe I could go to Guatemala for two weeks and return with a new stamp on my passport. No one would know. "No," he replied, "I keep my eye on these things. Going back is the right thing."

I was sinking, getting sadder and sadder by the second. "I promised you a year!"

"You'll have to finish it later," he said offhandedly.

If it was OK with the guru, then I guessed it was OK with me.

December: Return to the Ordinary World

> *We shall not cease from exploration, and the end of all our exploring will be to arrive where we started and know the place for the first time.*
>
> —*T. S. Eliot*

At the end of the adventure, the hero returns home, centered in a new state of being, which he shares with those around him.

My return to San Francisco held many surprises. Most of all was the new lens through which I saw the world. *Everything* looked new, bright, and colorful in ways I didn't know were possible. Working as a chef at the guru's stove was so much easier, my food quality so much better. I felt a strong connectedness with people I'd never felt before. The closer the relationship, the stronger and more harmonious the connectedness. Joy and love were my everyday emotional defaults. It was a beautiful December— and then came January, the start of another adventure, a new cycle.

THE UNIVERSALITY OF CYCLES

Although I labeled the phases of the journey's cycles as if each has a clear beginning and end, it is important to note that they don't really end. Instead, one phase flows into another, and one complete cycle flows into another, taking with it all that was gained in previous cycles. Their movement holds true to the definition of evolving; i.e., *to develop gradually from a simple to a more complex, refined form.*

When you engage, consciously, with an impassioned goal while observing the cycles' movements, evolving accelerates naturally.

Because the cycles are an ongoing force in the nature of human nature, we could say they are an organic, unseen body that causes humanity to evolve. Whether you are aware of your cycles or not, they are unfolding in your life, as they are in everyone's. That is because the cycles constitute a principle of human nature. You can identify a principle of human nature because it influences *every human being, everywhere in the world, throughout any time in history.*

Ask someone, anyone, anywhere in the world, at any time, to think about his or her life today: its conditions, the persons concerns for their loved ones today, where the person works, his or her age and children's ages, the car the individual drives, and so on. Next, ask the person to think back ten years and really zero in on who he or she was back then and what the conditions of life was like. Have the person consider as many details as possible, giving plenty of time to do so. Once the person is clearly focused ten years back in time with a real sense of who the person was then and what that lifestyle was like, ask the person to return to who he or she is today. Then ask, "Are you different now from who you were ten years ago"? The answer is nearly always *yes*! If you ask what caused the person to change, the answer is often vague. "Well, I don't know. I learned, I grew up, I evolved," is often along the lines of what you will hear.

For the average person, whose interests lie solely in a material life, the forces of human evolution are very subtle and influence his or her evolution very, very slowly. But for individuals with a desire for spiritual experience, or those with a desire to fulfill their soul's mission, evolutionary forces accelerate dramatically. If you are reading these words, you very likely fall into the second category. So get ready. The more you bring your awareness to the cycles, the more they speed up their enabling of your consciousness to expand; *expand* into your more authentic, higher human nature.

As the cycles accelerate, so does your process of inner purification. Inner purification simultaneously facilitates spiritual growth, the full details of which are covered in later chapters. But for now, know that inner purification is a steady letting go of all within yourself that is not of your Higher Self, of emotional wounds you may have suffered (often in childhood or adolescence), and of false beliefs you may harbor about what the nature of life is.

As to the true nature of life, let us say for now that it is underwritten by a benevolent force—the same force that creates the ebb and flow of the cycles. And here are a few other characteristics of this invisible force in life, or the "life within life," as I like to call it:

CHARACTERISTICS OF THE LIFE FORCE OF LIFE

- It embodies the Divine qualities of Goodness, Love, All-Knowing Wisdom, and Inspiration.
- It moves within its perfectly timed cycles, at the perfect level of intensity, which is always slightly higher than your present state of being.

- It triggers personal questioning about your life's direction.
- It's the source of inspirational thoughts that motivate inspired actions.
- It prods you into evolving at the crossroads of a new life direction.
- It prods your potential to flower.
- It breeds the ideas of a new life of possibility.
- It has always been and always will be there, invisibly supporting your life.
- It sweeps in and through you and through every human, world-wide, throughout all time.
- It's the reason behind the reason for life.
- Except for rare occasions, this Divine force communicates covertly to your subconscious—so you haven't known it's there until now.

The more you acknowledge this force, the more you will move in harmony with it. Paying attention to the cycles of your personal journey—while you continue to pursue Walt Baptiste's principles of meditation, yoga (or a similar discipline that heightens self-awareness), healthy eating, and physical fitness—is an excellent way to begin, and it assures your success.

MORE QUESTIONS

The year I described in this chapter was in 1976. I discovered Joseph Campbell's concept of the Hero's Journey ten years later. Seen through its lens, the events of 1976 and subsequent years fell into place with greater clarity. These were beautiful, exciting revelations—but I still had more questions. Many more questions! How do cycles inwardly affect the changes in us as humans? Clearly, they govern our internal change, but by what means? During the next two years, I was taught the answers.

In the remaining chapters, I will share with you the answers to my questions, sharing all you need to know about the inner purification process that paves the way to your self-mastery. In the next chapter, we will begin by taking a close look at the breaking-down process that is the result of a great interplay between the conscious and the subconscious mind.

5

How Your Mind Works

I'd like to begin this chapter with a moment of brutal honesty: the nature of the human condition is to create life out of the limits of the ego's subconscious conditioning—those "preloaded" programs that keep us divided and earthbound. Unless we can heal the wounds of our pasts and unless we can discover the *truth* of who we really are—by which I mean our authentic nature without our false beliefs—we have little hope of living our souls' visions of achieving our highest potential in this life cycle.

This brings us to a few important questions. How do we reduce the power of subconscious conditioning that insists on creating our life experiences like a broken record, repeating the same mistakes over and over? How can we give up our attachment to the memories, negative emotions, and false, unsubstantiated beliefs and opinions on which we base the reality of our lives and to which we are so yoked?

These are big questions that anyone could take a long time to ponder. For myself, the answer to experiencing a life of sustained happiness has been to free myself from the negatives of my past while developing a rich character of confident self-knowing. I've achieved it through a great deal of personal work and meditation that led to a well-informed understanding of the inner workings of *myself*. As I did, I found I was also learning the nature of human nature as well as the higher nature of Life itself. Most important, my understanding happened through the steady accumulation of one-step-at-a-time learning experiences over many years.

This chapter delivers the first step, which is to learn the differences among the various natures of the mind—the conscious mind, the subconscious mind with its support from the ego, the two types of memory, and the higher mental powers—as well as the role each plays during the functioning of our daily lives.

For our purposes, you don't need to go deep into the weeds of intellectual examination to understand your psychological makeup. Only the most basic understanding of the interplay between the subconscious mind and the conscious mind is required. Personally, this is all I have, and it's worked just fine for me for more than twenty years. If you're inspired to know more, an Internet search will yield in-depth information written in easy-to-understand language. Also, please bear in mind that describing the nature of anything means looking *generally* at how we find something to be. There are always exceptions when it comes to nature. Therefore, please understand that the following definitions of the nature of human psychology are based on the *overall* nature of the human condition.

THE CONSCIOUS AND SUBCONSCIOUS MINDS

A long time ago, back when car mufflers had to be replaced at least once during a vehicle's life-span, I found myself at the entranceway of a small, independent auto-repair shop. As I pulled in, a dark-eyed, wiry, thin man—not too tall, about five foot ten—approached me. He was holding a clipboard, ready to sign my car in for service. As I got out of my car, my first thought was, *I don't like this guy.*

That was just the beginning. The more questions he asked, recording my answers on his little clipboard, the more upset I became, until finally, my upset became anger—high levels of raging anger toward this young man, even though I didn't know him. At some point when we had finished our transaction, I said something very nasty to him and stormed off toward my girlfriend, who was waiting in her car to give me a ride back home. I jumped into the passenger seat, red hot, and slammed the door. My girlfriend asked, "Why are you so angry?"

"I hate that guy," I said.

She replied, " But you don't know him!" I was so upset, I couldn't respond. Instead, I sat there, staring out of the window, fuming with anger.

Why was I so angry with a perfect stranger? To get the answer to that question, we need to know something about the nature of human nature. More specifically, we need to know the nature of the minds. I use "minds" as a plural here because we have different areas of the mind—one is our conscious mind, with which we are all familiar, and the other is our subconscious mind. These two are very different and serve different functions. And there is a lot about the latter with which we are not really familiar at all.

Conscious Mind	Subconscious Mind
Logical, Analytical Thought	Irrational Reaction
Clear View of Outside World	Unfocused View of Outside World
Time Is Linear	Time Doesn't Exist
Access to Moral Compass	No Sense of Good or Evil
Access to Higher Mind	Ego-Based, Lower Mind
Limited Access to Memory	Instant Access to All Memory
Unaware of Subconscious Power	Powerful Sensing Capacity

Logical, Analytic Thought vs. Irrational Reaction
One of the main functions of the conscious mind is the ability to draw a logical conclusion from carefully considered information. Lacking in the ability to reason logically, *your subconscious mind will believe anything!* One of the subconscious mind's "jobs" is to prompt you into automatic, reactive responses based solely on your memories and unsubstantiated assumptions about your past and of life.

Clear View vs. Unfocused View of Outside World
Images of outside life pass through the lenses of the eyes and are then transferred via the optic nerve to a "screen"—the visual-cortex area of the brain—for viewing. As long as the lenses of the eyes are healthy, the mind interprets outside images with clarity. The subconscious mind doesn't have

direct access to the "screen." It's as if the subconscious is looking at blurred, out-of-focus images of the outside world from the back of the screen. What it sees when it looks at other people are general shapes of faces, shapes and postures of the body, style of hair, approximate ages, and so on.

Time Is Linear vs. Time Doesn't Exist

The conscious mind sees time as a progression of seconds moving in a linear direction. If I ask what you ate for lunch last Wednesday, the conscious mind believes it is looking back in time in order to remember last Wednesday's lunch. Likewise, if I ask what you will be doing at an appointment you have next Tuesday at 2:00 p.m., the conscious mind believes it is projecting into the future about what might be happening then. The subconscious mind, on the other hand, does not experience time. It experiences the memories of the past, the present, or imagined thoughts of the future in the context of the *now*.

Moral Compass vs. No Sense of Good or Evil

It is said that our definition of what constitutes moral behavior comes from the soul, with that feeling of ethical conscience we experience "*re-minding*" us to stop a hurtful behavior in a particular area of life and to realign our actions toward goodness. The higher one's evolution, the more sensitive one is to what constitutes moral behavior. In contrast, the subconscious mainly longs for two emotionally based experiences: being loved and feeling safe. As newborns, we are conditioned to believe that love is delivered to us from someone outside ourselves, namely our mother or father. During infancy, we are helpless to take care of our needs. Our first "belief" based on experience is that the people who give us constant attention by taking care of our every need are the gods who created the only world we know at this stage of life. Their attentive actions, whether positive *or* negative, are felt as experiences of life-preserving love. "If I gain the attention of my parent, then I exist" is the message we internalize. And our subconscious, lacking in its ability to logically deduce events, sees every act, loving or abusive, as verification that we are alive and valued.

As a child becomes more conscious of its small world, it enters a learning-by-observation mode, referencing the actions of parents and siblings to understand the rules of relationship behavior. Direct verbal signals are, of course, effective, but the deeper education comes from the child's observance of the parents' attitudes and behavior toward each other: what habits they demonstrate while relating to each other, and—even more interesting—how they relate to their friends and relatives. If the parents' natural habit of communicating with each other is imbued with loving tones and sweet attitudes (even when they argue, one can still hear undertones of love in their voices), the child will grow up with positive subconscious images of what marriage and family life are meant to be—and, as an adult, will seek to recreate the same positive home environment.

But let's say the opposite is true: that the two parents view their relationship as a power struggle, and every day engage in a barrage of loud, negative, argumentative language resulting in someone "winning " while the other spouse stews in the resentment of his or her loss. In this type of environment, there are three possible outcomes: 1) when the child grows up, its subconscious has been conditioned to believe that a negatively charged family environment is normal behavior, and he or she will duplicate the daily power-struggle arguments with his or her partner (and feel good about it, because to this person, power-struggle arguments are acts of love); 2) the child who is quite sensitive may decide to avoid marriage altogether because, to this person, marriage is a painful institution; 3) children with a more mature view of life, who sense for themselves the pain of an embattled relationship and vow to maintain their loving best while engaged in a marriage based on love will make the choice to participate in a relationship that is predicated on the answer to the question, "Does this person have a loving heart?"

The idea that the subconscious doesn't know the difference between right and wrong is clearly demonstrated when—and I hate to be too negative here, but this is, unfortunately, a not uncommon example—a child witnesses a parental relationship where one parent is an alcoholic and beats the spouse. As a result, we find the classic case in which that child grows up to marry an abusive alcoholic who beats him or her horribly, and that child not only refuses to leave the marriage but defends the spouse's right to beat him or her. Remember, the subconscious does not know the difference between right and wrong. All it wants is attention from "the one that loves me the most"—in this case, the abusive parent first, and by extension, the abusive spouse. (Those of you familiar with Sigmund Freud's work might recognize this as a "transference" dynamic, i.e., the inappropriate repetition in the present relationship of one that was important in a person's childhood.)

Higher Mind vs. Ego-Based. Lower Mind

Part of the conscious mind is consciousness itself. It's a point of pure energy located at what the East Indians have described as the center of the brain behind the eyes and labeled the *ajna* (or third-eye) center. Some say it is the location of the soul, while others say the soul is seated in the heart center. Personally, I don't know, so, as always when I haven't learned something from personal experience, I refer to whatever I've heard the guru say about a subject. "The eyes are the windows of the soul," Walt Baptiste often quoted. In one of his classes, he said, "If you could remove the pineal gland from a brain and look at it, you would see that it contains its own light." His language was not specific. But I still prefer to refer to the idea that the *ajna* center is the seat of the soul.

What experience *has* told me about this center is that the more I meditate at this point in the middle of my head, the more sustained conscious presence I experience (i.e., the real reality of life *minus* the subconscious beliefs and judgments of what I'm experiencing). Additionally, the *ajna* center is the receptor for the Higher Mind that Walt Baptiste also talked about. This Higher Mind brings to your awareness your higher perceptions, intuition, instinct, wisdom, and psychic insight (aka "knowing without knowing how you know").

The lower mind—what we commonly refer to as "gut instinct"—is centered mostly in a large complex of nerves (ganglia) located in the area of the solar plexus. The lower mind is ego based, hosting the ego's two main objectives: self-serving pleasure and security. The ego is the part of ourselves that determines what to allow into our lives: things that we believe will give us pleasure and that will keep us comfortably safe both from physical harm *and* from emotional harm (e.g., humiliation). The lower mind's choices for what constitute pleasure and safety are derived from the evidence of past experiences, and the ego is the enforcer of what is understood to be reality based on the evidence of the past. The ego builds a "comfort zone "style of life by choosing its environments, carefully avoiding the people and places that have in the past brought discomfort while selecting those that bring comfortable pleasure. Change is an enemy, as far as the ego is concerned. A mediocre life experience is the result of the ego's habit of clinging to what it believes is comfortable while avoiding the discipline required for giving up harmful habits.

Limited Access to Memory vs. Instant Access to All Memory
Another function of the ego is to scour the memories of past experiences to explain what is happening in the moment. Inside ourselves, believe it or not, we have two different types of memory. One type is like a file cabinet where we file things we know we will need to call forth later in life in order to function. The other style of memory is experiential memory.

Experiential memory is unique in that the subconscious observes situations in life and records, in fields of energy, everything that happens. For example, if I were to ask you what happened on your third birthday, you might say. "Well, gee, I'm forty years old. I have no idea." But your subconscious can recall your third birthday within a millisecond from your experiential memory, and it knows exactly what happened with crystal clarity. Was the day sunny or cloudy? Was your party inside or outside? Who were the children and adults who were there, and, most important, what emotions did you feel during your birthday party? If the entire party was a wonderful time for you, then the emotions of having a beautiful day are still there in experiential memory; if someone tried to steal a present from you and you angrily yanked it back out of his hands, then the brief moments of feeling anger toward that person is still in experiential memory. To the subconscious, "time" does not exist, so it believes your third birthday is happening right now.

All your life events—and especially the most important and emotionally impactful ones—are alive and unchanged inside your experiential memory, which is stored as energy fields within yourself. The fields of energy that make up experiential memory are spread throughout the body to the cells that are most aligned with the nature of each event. For example, let's say that as a child, you were praised over and over for being responsible (maybe as the oldest sibling, you willingly stepped up to take the parents' place when they were not around). Your parents praised you for being so mature and adult like. The energy of that experiential memory of praise for your responsible performance would then settle in the shoulder area. (The shoulders are the area in the body that holds responsibility. Remember the statue of Atlas with the world on his shoulders?) If you have a very positive memory of being a responsible child, you would find that, as an adult, your shoulders are healthy. If you do any strength training, you would find that the shoulders are unusually strong.

Now, let's say that the opposite was true. Let's say that when you were a child, your parents harped at you all the time, saying you were irresponsible, and because of your irresponsibility, you would never amount to anything. As an adult, you would find your shoulders weak, and you would have very little strength in that area. For another example, let's say, a woman walks in on her husband and his lover in their bed. Where is the first place that her hands go? They go right to the gut area—because the experiential memories having to do with family are centered in the lower gut, solar plexus, and sex-gland area.

Unaware of Subconscious Power vs. Powerful Sensing Capacity

Have you ever been in a public setting like a restaurant or a party and noticed that when a particular man steps into the room, your attention is ineluctably drawn to him, but you can't explain why? There is a compelling beauty about this person; you look and look but still can't quite put your finger on why. Or a person enters a crowded room, and your attention is drawn to that person, and you instantly know without having spoken to her that she is struggling because she has lost her emotional balance. You have just experienced the characteristic of the subconscious that has always been especially fascinating to me.

The subconscious cannot "see" the outside world, but it does have a talent for knowing about the people we encounter. Specifically, its talent is to reach out with an auric energy to "read" each individual in the immediate vicinity. It takes a reading on the energy field of the other person, whose subconscious is also taking the same sort of reading on us.

What is your energy field looking for in this situation? Three things. One is pleasure: "Will this person give me satisfaction?" Another is protection: "Is this person dangerous? Do I need to avoid him at all costs?" (This is why we sometimes find ourselves avoiding someone or literally walking around him or her, and we don't even know why.) And the last thing is connection. We want to know who people are! Our far-reaching auric energy loves the pleasure of getting to know people who have similar personalities and life experiences as ourselves, which explains the fun encounters we have when we talk to a stranger and it turns out we have a number of common connections—for example, we are friends with the same people or once worked for the same company. ("Like attracts like" is the expression supplied to us by the Law of Attraction.)

Here is an experience I had when I learned about the nature of our subconscious to form an opinion about people around us. On occasion, Walt Baptiste had a series of meditation classes on Friday evenings. They would start late and end late. One particular time, late on a dark winter evening, as I left class and drove through the quiet streets of San Francisco on my way to the freeway entrance, I began to realize that I was really, really calm from the meditation class. Physically, mentally, and emotionally, every part of myself felt a beautiful, harmonious calm. I remember that I did not want to look around or turn my head left or right; I just wanted to maintain my posture and maintain this wonderful sense of calm and well-being.

I approached a stoplight that turned yellow and then red, and as I stopped, just basking in this wonderful feeling of peace, I saw out of the corner of my eye that an individual had stepped up to the curb and was waiting for the "walk" light, which meant the person was going to walk in front of my car. But I didn't want to turn and look at this person; I didn't want the distraction. I was still feeling how great it was to be so calm, when the image of a young girl I'd gone to high school with fifteen years earlier popped into my mind. My immediate thought was, *What? Why am I envisioning this girl after all these years?* I didn't know why—because I hadn't given her a thought since the last time I had seen her at graduation. But there it was, the image of her, clear as a bell, in my head, as were the emotions I'd felt toward her, which were sweet because I had always been a bit smitten with her.

Just then, the "walk" light turned for this individual, and she started across the street. As I looked at her, I could see that her age, face, hairstyle, and body type all were very similar to those of the girl I'd just thought of. And perhaps, if I had gotten to know this individual, she would have turned out to have the same pleasing disposition that my high-school friend had had. This was a great experience for me. Because of it, I was made aware that my subconscious has the capacity to reach out with its energy field and read the energy fields of individuals in my environment.

Now, let's return to my unprovoked anger with the gentleman at the muffler-repair shop. Stay with me while I circle back to this: when I was a small, thin six-year-old, my large extended family had a big family reunion. It was a picnic at a park, and a lot of people were there: uncles, aunts, cousins, and second cousins—many of whom I'd never met before. Among the relatives was a cousin around nineteen or twenty who found joy in hurting people in any way he could. He was also very clever at it. He would find me, and even in the midst of a big group of people, he had a very shrewd way of discerning the precise moment when no one was looking at us. At that moment, he would reach out and squeeze my earlobe and twist it like crazy, causing me to wince with pain. He would turn away at the precise instant when someone might see us.

My efforts to avoid him were to no avail. He would always find me and do it again, or else he'd smack my shoulder with his fist, or he'd grab my neck like he was going to choke me. Again, he would stop just at the moment we were about to be seen. After several of these abuses, he leaned over and whispered in my ear, "If you tell anybody what I've done to you, I'm going to hurt your sister far worse than I've hurt you." Well, my sister was four! But the tone of his voice was so dark that I knew he meant it, so I didn't say anything.

The next year, I was seven, and family-reunion time came around. Everyone had said they'd had such a great time at the last one that we should do it again. So we did—and there was this kid. He came up to me, and as he did, I was overcome by a powerful surge of overwhelming anger, both because he was there and because he could pull off his habit of hurting people and get away with it. I was also frightened that he was going to hurt my sister if I said anything. So I did everything I could to avoid him and took the hits when I couldn't.

After that day, thank goodness, I never saw him again. If I were asked to describe him, I would say he was a really thin, wiry guy with black hair and deep-set, dark eyes—just like the guy with the clipboard checking me in at the muffler shop! And perhaps if I had gotten to know this fellow, I would have found that he also had within his character a mean streak that found joy in hurting other people. That day at the shop, my conscious mind was seeing a total stranger, but the subconscious reading I took on this person reminded me (by looking at his "blurred outline"—face, hair, age, posture, and so on—and drawing on my experiential memory) of my cousin. My unconscious actually believed that this young man *was* my cousin, so I began to react with overwhelming levels of anger that resided in the field of my experiential memory—anger that had been placed there years earlier when I was six and seven years old.

RETURNING TO WHOLENESS

So, here we have examples of how the subconscious and the conscious minds function with different characteristics for different purposes. We all carry with us as adults these fields of experiential energy that contain everything of importance that happened to us, both positive and negative—the positive moments when we felt seriously loved and the negative moments when we were horribly physically or emotionally wounded. Despite the skill of the unconscious at identifying people who stir up our experiential memories of pleasure and pain, it's these experiential memories themselves that stand in the way of our wholeness.

The interplay between the conscious and subconscious minds is vitally important to understand while participating in the inner purification process. If, from your inner witness, you consciously "see" yourself reacting to someone or something in the moment it's happening and you know your reacting source is coming from a specific childhood conditioning, you are already on the right path. The mere act of consciously witnessing your angst with compassion, i.e., with the "light" of your conscious observation, does, to a small degree, reduce the energy field of experiential memory. Instead of succumbing (going subconscious) to the habit of reacting defensively, which adds to the energy of the field, you have instead healed: reduced, to some degree, the experiential memory along with its energy to dictate your life choices.

For example, as a child, I was one of those high-energy, quick-witted kids. My mind was very active, and I had the habit of coming up with what I thought were "bright ideas." My bright ideas often were the result of my ability to see beyond obvious limitations and come up with alternate possibilities, whereas my parents passively gave up. Yes, I was very innocent, and often, my thoughts reflected the innocence of youth, but my ideas also reflected a real intelligence. Because of their insecurity, though, my parents felt threatened. Their many typical responses, repeated thousands of times to repress my thinking, could be boiled down to one message: "You're stupid. Stop saying stupid things." If I questioned their retorts, their answer was, "Because you sound stupid." If I persisted with another *why*, then I'd hear the usual, "Because I said so. *Now, shut up!*" And, finally, if I continued by speaking up to defend my position, the result was a slap across the face.

What was the result of the barrage of parental disapproval on my desire to help with what I believed to be "bright ideas"? As an adult, whenever I was among peers, and especially among strangers, I was an observer rather than a participant (which has its advantages). In any situation where I was about to say something that exposed to people the intelligent side of who I really was, I stopped myself and held back. Teaching something that was personal to me, such as yoga, in public classes, to people I didn't know, was out of the question. However, when I did decide that it was time to share with others what I knew about yoga and meditation, I had to inwardly agree to face my fears of exposing who I am on a deeper, more personal level, through my *voice, to strangers*!

In the beginning, I had a lot of fear—so much fear that, while guiding people through the yoga postures, my voice shook. If a woman with the same powerfully negative judgmental outlook on life that my mother had had ever entered the yoga room, I would shake violently with fear in my gut area (the subconscious reaches out to "read" the character of the people you encounter). Yet each experience of fear was a blessing. It was an opportunity to continue exposing who I really am while residing in the witness aspect of myself, thus reducing the experiential cloud that had programmed me to believe I would feel the pain of rejected love if I spoke from the truths of my unique self. Today, my fear in such situations is gone, replaced with the joy of giving service to people through yoga.

I never attended college-level social-science courses to learn human psychology. Instead, the information was delivered to me as it always is: through pieces of experience. The first piece of information was the discovery of the cycles during the beginning years of working at the Hungry Mouth Restaurant. Next came a period of time, right around year ten of working at the stove, when I went through three-plus months of a steady flow of recurring memories, recalling the events of my childhood cycling through my mind. The result was a deep understanding of how I had been molded by certain beliefs about myself as well as an understanding of my parents' psychological profiles. I saw how they were conditioned by *their* environment and life experiences and why they responded to life the way they did as adults. I realized why my mother was so paranoid about safety and security.

When my mother was eight, her mother was struck and killed by lightning; when she was thirteen, her father died of cancer. Her oldest brother, twenty-one at the time, was supposed to provide for his four siblings but never really did. As an adult, my mother was obsessed with a need for security. My father, riding a mercurial roller coaster of mood swings, was cold emotionally because his father was cold emotionally. My sister and I suffered through countless beatings from our father because his father beat him. Both parents saw life through the lens of a negative self-image and believed that the world offered little in the way of safety or security. As a result, they took the frustrations of their fear-based subconscious motives out on us in the form of physical abuse (by our father) and even more damaging emotional abuse (by our mother).

The next piece of understanding was given to me four years later when I discovered the storytelling stages of the Hero's Journey from Joseph Campbell. I was thrilled to learn that the cycles of energy I had experienced while working at the stove were the same as its stages. In fact, I was ecstatic at the discovery, but I lacked the reason that I had been given the experiences. I needed more information.

During the following eighteen months, I was filled with a passion to read as many books on human psychology and mythology as I could get my hands on. During that experience, I was amazed to find that I understood the complicated psychological reasoning easily because of the previous revelations concerning my family history while working at the stove. One day, a man started a conversation with me in my favorite café. "I see you in here often," he said, "reading books by Sigmund Freud and Carl Jung. Are you a psychology student?" His question was the beginning of his mentorship of me. As a man with a doctorate in psychiatry, he was well qualified to tutor me, proving the expression, "When the student is ready, the teacher appears."

There came a time in my training when I was still very unsure of my knowledge. My mentor tried to convince me otherwise with repeated comments like, "You know more than you think you know," but to no avail. My reluctance to believe him vanished after he sent me to a lecture by Dr.

Stephen LaBerg, a famous lucid-dream researcher at Stanford University. LaBerg began his lecture by defining the different areas of the conscious and subconscious minds and the inner roles they play in our lives. Yes, my face wore a big smile as his words confirmed *everything* I had just learned over the past year and a half.

Finally, the last important piece of information came to me during my "above the world" experience. I returned with the connective realization that the purpose for the force of the cycles is to heal our past wounding while strengthening our character. The combination of all my experiences verified that wisdom comes experientially.

PURIFYING EMOTIONAL WOUNDS

We are all programmed with the energetic fields of emotional wounds and false, unsubstantiated ideas that inform what we believe life to be. We are molded positively by parents who are open, happy, gregarious connecters with lots of friends or negatively by parents who mistrust people and life. We are shaped by parents who always speak in loving tones to each other or by parents who are focused on power struggles. It's all there in the experiential memory: the people who were involved, along with crystal-clear imagery of each event. And your ego believes the events are alive, happening in this very moment.

As an adult, the more you purify the emotional wounds, the more you surrender your unsubstantiated, conditioned beliefs of the past while trading them for the Truth (shifting the real from the unreal, as Walt Baptiste used to say). The more you naturally live from your higher soul nature, the more you come alive in the spiritual nature of yourself and of life. As your passion to know more deepens through process, you are naturally attracted to the higher teachers you will need, and they to you.

Here's the kicker. Your subconscious is a powerful creator. It is far more powerful at creating your life than you reasoning mind is. Most of the time, people create from their lower energy centers (chakras)—unconsciously, without direction or self-awareness. That is why they repeat life like a broken record, playing the same patterns with the same scenarios and the same mistakes, over and over. It's the contents of your experiential memories that keep you from the freedoms and joys of your higher humanity and your higher Self. This is what I realized that day as I stared out of my car window in the experience I described in chapter 2. I saw the full extent of my negative subconscious paradigms formed by the toxic family life I had experienced while growing up. Because those experiential memories were alive and functioning in the creating of my family life as an adult, I was not free to be who I really am. My response was to make a deep, heartfelt commitment to free myself from *all* of it. I had mastered being a chef; I had uncovered my unique genius—my unique understanding of what it means to live life engaged as the whole human. Now I was going to master my soul's life lesson.

If in the chapter 3 exercises you wrote out your deepest desires with great emotion, there is a strong possibility that your soul's concerns are in there somewhere. Most often, your soul's needed experience is in the one area that you have the most passion to resolve, be it your life lesson or the development of your unique talent. The fact remains—because you *meant* it when you wrote it, and you are ready to take a specific action toward resolving an emotional issue or mastering a talent—you will find Spirit accelerating its synchronistic help in increasingly noticeable ways. In fact, because of your deep, committed sincerity, your guiding Divine Support is already busy arranging those events, one at a time, in perfect order for you *right now!*

But guess what? There is yet another dynamic you need to contend with.

SURPRISE, SURPRISE

This chart demonstrates what happens inside you when you say with passion, "I can see the goal, the vision of a better life, and I absolutely won't stop until I live it!"

The increase of your purposeful actions will flush to the surface any of your internal negative beliefs that are directly opposed to where you intend to go.

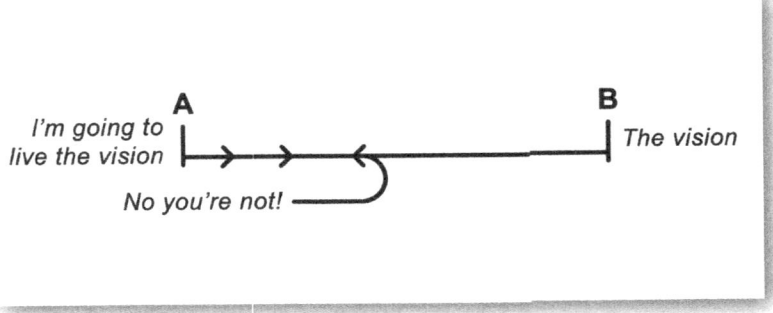

For every positive action you take, the ego, along with the forces of the subconscious, will meet it with an equal and opposite negative force—an *equal and opposite force* that constitutes inner resistance. It's as if the subconscious is saying, "No! You're not going that way!" This force is made up of your ego's lower-programmed, negative beliefs of what you think life is and your conditioned beliefs about who you are meant to be. It's the part of your ego that refuses to let go of something it believes is vitally important to keep in place, even if it is wrong. In Joseph Campbell's language, you've stepped into the Reluctant Hero state of being.

If you meet your negative unconscious force with increased will, forcing things to happen, your subconscious will quietly sabotage success in surprisingly subtle ways *with an equal force*. At the completion of one whole cycle, you will find yourself frustrated and back at your starting point. Regrettably, I rode on that merry-go-round for two years before the experience that gave me the principles defined in this book.

But don't take my word for it. Once you have agreed to hold deep integrity while taking full responsibility for your life, followed by committed action toward the vision of your goal, you'll quickly find a myriad of negative reasons why *you can't succeed* racing to the surface of your consciousness. Try to force progress by adding a lot of will to fulfill the vision, and watch the negative forces within yourself rise up to meet the positive actions of your increased will: *force for force*!

So, what is the answer to overriding your ego's negative opposing force? There must be a second positive force that joins with your positive committed actions to neutralize the force of your resistance. When the two positive forces join, they become the impetus for transformation—a transformation that initiates the inner realizations that expose your more authentic nature.

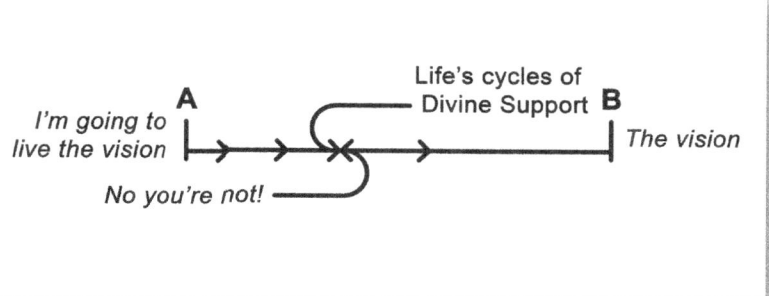

What is that second force? It is the rhythms of the cycles of Life itself supporting your very real desire for internal change on your way to self-mastery. The beauty of the process *is* the *eternal reliability* of the movement of the forces within the cycles, cycling round and round, healing your attachments to the past while revealing the truths of yourself: Truths of Life and Spirit. The energies flowing within the form place you in orchestrated events, or they bring to you thoughts of Truth about healing and about who you really are. With each cycle, you are lighter and happier while evolving steadily toward a higher human life experience.

Another beautiful thing about the Life Force within Life that is supporting you is that it is Divine in nature. One of the real joys when using Life as your guide is in those moments of discovering how Life is magically (or maybe I should say *miraculously*) intelligent. There are those moments when it is clear that Spirit knows all of your secrets, all the negative experiential memories that stand in the way of fulfilling your highest soul's vision and that must be healed. This Divine nature of Life sees *all* of what is inside you, and It knows the exact events and the exact order of the events that you need to experience in life in order to neutralize your negative history, one step at a time.

Old programming and the need to release it *is* both the inner reason *for* Life and also the gift *of* Life in this realm of existence. That is what I mean when I refer to "the reason behind the reason for life."

I don't doubt that at this point, you might feel like a lot of my students have: overwhelmed—as you realize just how much within yourself needs to be healed. My suggestion to you is to think long term. What we are describing here really is a lifelong pursuit. Decide that it's worth it. The result is an amazing, new, vital life adventure.

A RECAP ON THE SUBCONSCIOUS

In summary, here are some important things to remember about the subconscious:

First, depending on your level of consciousness, a huge percentage of your choices arise from what your subconscious believes life is meant to be. As soon as you believe as fact what you are told from *any* outside source, a paradigm is formed that creates your decisions and behavior. So many of the dramas that you repeat over and over are merely your unsubstantiated ego-based paradigms creating scenarios to confirm your false assumptions.

The rub is in the fact that the *lower-personality nature* of your subconscious is the powerhouse that creates your life experiences from experiential memory—until you form the habit of listening (actually, *sensing* is a better word) inside for the authentically truthful answers to your every question. By using your conscious mind and the transformation process you are now engaged in, you can heal and neutralize the original beliefs.

Second, the subconscious is like another person within yourself that you can develop a relationship with. When you are hurting, you can ask it what the problem is, and it will usually, though not always, give you the answer in the form of a thought or image or both. If it doesn't answer, often your Higher Self will provide the answer in its infinite array of life experiences.

This is where meditation is a major help. The practice of meditation develops and refines "space" between the conscious and subconscious. You become used to the difference between how your lower subconscious and your Higher Self each provide answers. The sound and feel of them are different. For example, let's say you find thirty e-mails in your inbox. As you scan through them, taking care not to delete something of importance, you find that twenty-five of them are truly junk, but you are not sure about the other five. You are about to delete those anyway when the subject line of one catches your eye—and for good reason. You open it and find that its contents describe in detail the elements of a problem you have been struggling with and didn't know how to resolve. As you read, a solution comes to mind, and along with it, the relief of finally realizing exactly what you need to do.

The question is, why did you open the e-mail? Because the impulse to do so was there. There was a brief but clear, impulsive feeling of a personal connection to the contents of the e-mail accompanied with a "knowing" (*claircognizance*) that it was important to you on a very personal level as none of the others were. The sound and feel of the words of the subject line were more pronounced than the usual ramblings of your subconscious dialogue.

You can develop this sense of differentiation with steady meditation. A thankful acknowledgment of an answer from your Higher Self delivers a moment of focused love toward those inner gifts from Spirit. The more you acknowledge the Spirit's gifts of answers to your questions—sometimes even the most seemingly unimportant questions—the more Spirit will, in turn, give you answers. This is because whatever you focus on expands.

Third, the ego, along with its relationship with the subconscious, maintains the false premise that all love and happiness come from people or events outside of you. This false premise tells you that you'll find happiness only when:

- Somehow, you make a parent love and accept you
- You are liked by all others, or you are irresistible to the opposite sex
- You have the money to make other people envious of you and your lifestyle

The ego also falsely believes that your happiness depends on others changing their behavior. So you imagine that you will be happy *if only my partner would stop being mean*, or *if only my partner would pay my way in life*.

These kinds of ego-driven achievements are illusory and pose hindrances to any chance at discovering the Truths of Reality and genuine, lasting happiness.

Here, again, meditation is the answer. Meditation develops your self-awareness and sensitivity to the *truth or reality* of the moment to a highly refined degree. Your talent for observing your thoughts and consciously choosing which to respond to and which to ignore refines your character. Your choices become love based as your will to Good strengthens.

The next chapter, "The Living Process," describes the flow of life's energies that clear the emotional wounds and false, conditioned beliefs of the experiential memories that block not only the truth of who we are but also the higher realities of Life. Processing exposes these greater Truths while serving your desire for a life of soul fulfillment and spiritual experience. Additionally, you will learn how I process through life itself, *daily*, with my desire to fulfill my soul's destiny.

6

The Living Process

During the long downturn in my life, I was stuck in the beliefs that represented my own mother's voice: "You can't do anything right. You'll never amount to anything; you're just plain stupid. You will always be poor. You are going to die alone, homeless, in the street." This loop of fatalistic presentiment repeated literally thousands of times.

Even though I had proven otherwise while working for my guru, I was still immersed in a state of ignorance—unable to create successfully out of my own strengths. My connection to and trust in Higher Self had once again become submerged. Instead, I made choices based solely on the negative childhood beliefs that had been drummed into me.

During that time, subconscious motivations of self-sabotage determined my life path. I took jobs that would never cover my living expenses. Three times, I joined companies that ended up closing their doors less than a year later. As my unemployment benefits ran out, my credit-card debt swelled. All too often, I found myself talking to collection agents asking me when they could expect payment. At first, I learned the best way to play the game with them so as not to ruin my credit. But then I thought, *Why learn to play that game?* Get a job. Get a good job, the right job. That wasn't happening, though, because the higher energy that was so much a part of my real self was not flowing through me or through my life. Thankfully, the energies of inner purification, which is where my focus was strongest during this period, flowed steadily. Beneath the surface, I was surrendering, one at a time, the tensions around old childhood programs put in place by my early family environment.

That all changed the morning of the one defining moment when I screamed, "Enough!" In that moment, the memory of my strength and creative power returned. I reconnected with it by recalling the genuine strength I'd demonstrated while working for Walt Baptiste and realizing that that strength was still there inside of me. In that instant, a powerful internal energy was set free. From that point forward, my life path was more spiritually infused, and the "real Walter" began to emerge. A few months later, I began working with my first private client. The real me was showing up, and I was *accepting him*!

There were still many years of purification ahead, but I met them with a much greater confidence. I knew, and still know, exactly where I am at any given moment in the cycles. I know exactly what it is that I'm working on, as well as where my character is strengthening, maturing, and evolving. I handle the tensions with more ease. My periods of listening to "informing wisdom" are deeper, richer, and more filled with joy.

I want to be clear. I wouldn't change the hard years for anything. They enabled me to appreciate the love, joy, and freedom from anxious worry that I experience today.

THE GOOD LIFE

Your Good seeks you even as you seek your Good.

—*WALT BAPTISTE*

Dozens of times, I'd heard Walt repeat the above expression. Over the years, I have been blessed to learn many wonderful truths during the "living process" of inner purification and spiritual growth—one of them being the nature of Spirit's/God's *sustained force of love* is forever aimed at giving us what we want and more. I've also learned that when I'm not experiencing the perfection of the heavenly life meant for me, it's because the negative energies I still hold somewhere inside me are blocking, or pushing away, the gifts of the Divine.

How can you give up your attachment to the memories, the emotions, the false beliefs and opinions on which you base the reality of your life and to which you remain so attached? How do you reduce the power of the subconscious conditioning that creates your life experiences like a broken record, repeating the same mistakes over and over? The answer is to immerse yourself in the life behind life, the "living process."

Synchronicity: the unfolding of events that are meaningful coincidences.

The "living process" is the path that spirit, as guru, guides us along. The term refers to the invisible path, the orchestrated, synchronistic events that teach us, that lead us, that are meant to heal us—one step at a time—until we have achieved success in our souls and spiritual pursuits. The resulting success is a life of True Wealth: *a wealth of rich human character traits and rich, vibrant life experiences* as well as material wealth.

This chapter describes some of the different forms of events that Spirit provides for the inner healing of our pasts while guiding us through our souls' accelerated evolution. The following story is a case in point. It illustrates an area of my life where I was holding a lot of misguided images and shows how the inner purification process worked to clear away the negative energies of those deep, long-held false beliefs.

A KARMA OF THE HEART

Some years ago, while I was settling comfortably into my seat at my favorite movie theater, waiting for a film to begin, I realized that I wasn't feeling so well. Then I realized I was breathing heavily and becoming warm and sweaty. My attention was really piqued when my heart began racing and I started gasping for breath. I didn't know what the problem was, but I was sure it would pass. Well, it didn't—and after ten minutes, I drove myself to the nearest hospital, where I was admitted for testing.

Three days later, Dr. S calmly told me that I had congenital heart disease. When I asked what that meant, he said, "You have a leaky aortic valve that needs to be replaced, as well as an enlarged heart."

As someone who has used nutrition many times in the past to heal health problems, the first question I asked Dr. S was, "Can the heart valve heal itself with the right nutrition?"

"No, it needs to be replaced," he answered.

"Really?" I replied, not actually believing him. I had jumped to my usual attitude of, "We'll see about that," and, "Watch me prove you wrong."

Dr. S, sensing I wasn't grasping the seriousness of the situation, said, "With our testing instruments, we can determine the amount of blood pumped from the heart with each heartbeat. The measurement term used is the *ejection fraction*. Normal ejection fraction numbers are 50 percent to 70 percent. An ejection fraction reading of 65 means that 65 percent of the total amount of blood in the left ventricle, the main pumping chamber, is pumped out to perform its many functions with each heartbeat. Any reading below 40 percent indicates a problem in the heart and needs to be attended to. The lower the number, the greater the chance of a sudden cardiac arrest.

"Your ejection fraction is 18 percent," he added casually. Needless to say, that got my attention. "You need surgery. But I won't be the one doing it," Dr. S went on. "I'm going to refer you to Dr. D, a cardiac surgeon at [a nearby county hospital]."

Ten days later, I left Dr. D's office after a two-and-a-half-hour consultation, worried and anxious. There was something amiss. I wasn't comfortable with what this doctor was suggesting or with his hesitation to commit to doing the surgery. In other words, he failed to gain my confidence. He closed our meeting by saying he wanted to talk with Dr. S and have the test results sent to his office. He would call me when he had them.

My concerns were heightened by the fact that this is not the way my life had typically flowed. Why weren't the right solutions making themselves available to me? I must have been blocking life's flow of energy.

Two more weeks passed with no response from Dr. D, so I called him and left messages…no callbacks! When he finally did respond, he proposed a surgery that would result in a very debilitating, impractical result that would limit my movement for the rest of my life. Hearing this, I was left with even less confidence in his advice and recommendations.

With an ejection fraction of 18 percent, both doctors had said that the quicker I could have the valve fixed, the better. Dr. D hadn't worked out, but as I hung up the phone, I wasn't panicked—even though, truthfully, I didn't know where to turn next. That didn't matter. What mattered to me was the strong "knowing" I had that it was not my time for death, and that no matter what it took, I'd find health again. I also knew that my heart problem was a wake-up call of some sort, and I was going to find out what that was about.

Knowing I was being completely looked after by Spirit, I watched for signs of what to do next. I was sure that combing the Internet for the right surgeon would lead me instinctively to the right person for the job. Alas, I searched and searched, but no doctor's name sparked an intuitive hit. As more days passed and still nothing came, either from the outside or intuitively from the inside, I felt a deep sense of being lost, empty, and forgotten. In desperation, I turned to longer meditations while asking what to do. *Still nothing*!

I'm the type of person who likes to be as self-sufficient as possible. I keep my problems to myself and never ask people for help, knowing that the answer to any problem is somewhere within myself. But as the days turned into weeks, I came to understand that the reason I wasn't being given the answers I needed was that I had to put my pride aside and reach out to ask for help.

The moment after I had that realization, I had a thought to contact Dr. Wade Smith, an orthopedic surgeon, student of Walt Baptiste, and a very close friend of mine. After I detailed the problem, his first comment threw me off balance: "Why have you thrown up a wall against doctors?"

His question triggered the realization of just how much tension I was holding—by choice—that I didn't have to suffer. Inwardly, I questioned myself: *Why would I want to reject a doctor's help?*

I didn't respond to Wade's question. He pressed further: "The heart has a way of strengthening itself when it needs to, but valves are like plumbing. You've got to get a plumber to switch out the broken valve for a new one." That also got my attention. My friend was confirming what Dr. S., the first doctor I had dismissed so offhandedly, had said. *OK*, I thought, *this is more serious than I imagined*. With each piece of information, I could feel my inner negative tensions letting go little by little.

Wade's advice was to find a good heart surgeon, one who also thought more like me, and schedule a consultation. The next day, he gave me a list of ten good potential candidates, and to that I added five doctors I had found. They all practiced cardiac surgery along with integrative medicine, touting such services as mindful meditation and yoga as part of their practices. It took me nearly a week to call them all. *None* of them worked out, for various legitimate reasons.

In frustration, I temporarily gave up the search. The problem of who the right surgeon was would have to be taken care of, as I knew it would be, by Spirit. For now, I needed a deeper understanding of my part in keeping life's Higher Life stream at bay. When I concentrated on the problem, several reasons came to mind. In the part of myself, emotional and attitudinal, that was not taking responsibility for the fix, I was avoiding facing certain realities— i.e., the magnitude of the situation. On a deeper, subtler level, I was holding on to the idea that I could fix the heart through nutrition and meditation, without doctors. I was also harboring a very old program that told me that doctors were to be avoided at all costs—especially when it came to being cut open. Also, at the time of my diagnosis, I had just decided I was more ready than ever to begin helping people on a larger, more public scale. Now I was resentful that, because of a heart problem, I was not able to begin my most meaningful work. And last, there was inertia. I dreaded giving my energy to something other than what *I* wanted to do.

Next, I received an e-mail reminder from Wade that my problem was a "karma of the heart" that had to be resolved. And to resolve it without creating more karma was to take action without holding a conditional outcome in mind: no preconceptions, no actions of the ego. Of course, I knew about action without attachment to outcomes, but when I read his words, I was immediately surprised at the amount of doubtful tension I was feeling related to the idea that I wouldn't be successful in locating the right doctor. That realization was followed with an instant, deep, healing surrender.

More time passed as I resumed the search, again to no avail, for the right doctor: someone with a solution that sounded practical, someone I could believe in. Meditation and prayer became more important than ever. Truthfully, in my prayers, I was appealing to Walt Baptiste for a miraculous healing, hoping to avoid the messy uncertainty of heart surgery altogether. It wasn't working. I was getting sicker.

Then, in a phone conversation, Wade asked, "How does a surgeon get the knowledge and skill to help? Through God's grace…so if a surgeon or doctor can help you, why is that not a gift from God?" Honestly, my surrender as he spoke those words was profoundly deep, accompanied with the powerful realization that my prayer had been answered in its own way. This was exactly what I had been looking for. This was the last piece of information I needed to give up all feeling of fear and the angst-filled thoughts that told me the problem was not going to be solved perfectly— the right way, the "freeing of the heart karma" way.

A few days later, I found two paragraphs in one of Walt Baptiste's publications describing the importance of addressing a karma issue of the body, which appears to go very deep. It showed just how critical it is to take up the "right attitude" for seeing our karmas through: a positive, proactive attitude. Here's part of what he wrote:

There are great souls who radiate soul-qualities through bodies racked with pain, arthritis and cancers, but it is not to the credit of that person however saintly and fortunate enough to be of such measure of soul. In the next incarnation this great soul-person will have to care for the BODY, or the Soul that is given on the way up or the "spirituality" will be taken away again.

Yes! Now I was free of any negatives holding back life's flow, keeping life's gifts at bay. In fact, the opposite became the case: I was filled with determination to regain my health—whatever was required. In fact, I was even looking forward to embarking on the adventure as the hero in my own life. Later, I ran across these words: "Everything of worth has its cost."

Repairing the heart certainly was of great worth to the rest of my life; it offered a real second chance, and I was going to pay whatever costs were required.

During this time, a carpenter came to my house to install a set of much-needed double-pane windows in the living room. The morning after I had read Walt's words, the carpenter asked me to grab a box full of tools that I was walking past. I said, "I'm sorry, but I'm sick and don't have the strength to lift it"—even though the box wasn't that heavy.

"Sick?" he exclaimed, surprised, "You don't look sick. What's the problem?" I told him I had something wrong with my heart. "What do you need? Is it a heart-valve replacement?" he asked.

"Yeah," I said. Now I was the one surprised.

"Have you decided which kind of valve you want to replace your leaking one? Will it be an organic pig valve, or a mechanical valve?"

I just stood there silently, looking at this six-foot, five-inch-tall carpenter standing in front of me with his work boots, exposed skinny legs clad in shorts, a nail apron, and a hammer in his hand, asking what type of heart-replacement valve I had chosen to replace my leaking valve. My face must have registered a dumbfounded look, because he laughed.

"My mother had one of those operations twenty years ago," he said. "She chose the pig valve, because with the mechanical valve, you're stuck taking Coumadin [a blood thinner that is known to have unpleasant side effects] for the rest of your life."

"That's good to know. Thanks for the tip," I said as I began to walk away. (Truthfully, I had had no idea there were two types of valves; neither that I had to choose which one I wanted.)

"You know," the carpenter said to my back, "I don't have much faith in those [county hospital] surgeons." My instincts jumped to attention again. I hadn't said a word about a county hospital. And it wasn't what he said, but the sound of his voice as he said it. He continued as I turned to face him again with the same dumbfounded expression. "They had already opened her chest to fix the valve, but six months later, when she wasn't feeling right, they were going to open her up again! That just seemed wrong to me. Luckily, I found the greatest heart surgeon in the country, right here in the Bay Area. When I explained the problem to the good doctor, he said, 'You bring her to me.' He prescribed a few medications for her, and in four weeks, she was fine."

"What's the doctor's name?" I asked, almost yelling. *He couldn't remember!*

"Give me some time. I'll come up with it," he promised.

An hour later, he handed me a piece of paper with a name on it: Dr. Vincent Gaudiani.

I was positive this was the gift I'd been looking for. As I Googled the name, my mind raced through questions like, "Twenty years ago, he helped the carpenter's mother, but is he still practicing? Is he even still alive? And, if so, has he retired? *Yes, yes,* and *no* were the answers. He was still practicing nearby in Redwood City, California.

I wasn't ready yet to get excited about the possibility of finding the perfect surgeon. Instead, I was anxious when I called Dr. Gaudiani's office simply to find out if he accepted my insurance. The nice woman on the other end of the line said he did, and without skipping a breath asked, "Do you want an appointment with Dr. Gaudiani? I can fit you in Wednesday at 1:30 p.m. Can you be here at that time?" Yes, I could, and found myself sitting across from the good doctor two days later. In twenty minutes, he conveyed so much confidence that any doubt I might have had that he was the right surgeon for the job vanished. And there it was: I had opened to the flow of Life's movement once again.

The operation was successful, and four weeks after being released from the hospital, I visited Dr. Gaudiani for a follow-up examination. By all the indications, I was recovering better than expected. "I'm going to refer you back to Dr. S now, your original cardiologist. Schedule your next thirty-day follow-up with him. If you have questions, call him." On my way out, Dr. Gaudiani said, "By the way, say hello to Dr. S for me." So it seemed that he knew Dr. S.

Four weeks later, I was in the office of Dr. S with my son Tyler for another follow-up appointment. As I was leaving, I mentioned that Dr. Gaudiani had asked me to say hello and that it sounded like they knew each other. "Oh, yes," said Dr. S. "We are very good friends. We worked together for ten years in San Jose."

On the way to the car, Tyler asked, "If they are such good friends, why the hell didn't he recommend Dr. Gaudiani in the first place?"

My immediate answer was, "Because I had to go through the adventure of finding him."

Simple, everyday coincidences? Or a series of synchronistic, meaningful events? What do *you* think?

A MAGNET FOR THE GOOD

During your writing exercises, you engaged *all* of yourself while looking back, followed by a serious examination of your potential for an ideal future. The road to resolving these polarities—the freedom from a conditioned past, along with success in creating a desired future—is paved, brick by brick, by a conscious *engagement* in the present. Movement along that road is determined by your *level of commitment* while taking your actions, which keeps the energies of the "living process" flowing.

Being mindful is not the same as being present; it's simply the part that the mind plays while your entire being is established in "presence." Presence is a state of being. What Walt Baptiste called "living process" occurs when you are present *in consciousness*, witnessing life from your observer, with your authentic being and all your senses—including smell, hearing, and sensing the energies of a person or an environment—engaged in the act of being present. You will especially enjoy the benefit of the "living process" when you take impassioned, committed action toward an ideal future. The experiences the creative force brings *are healing your past while supporting your success.*

The inner-purification/psychological-maturity process occurs naturally in life primarily on the subconscious level. Your good efforts now will serve to bring the process to the conscious level by intuitively sensing its forces and witnessing its flow consciously. One of the great side effects of meditation (right meditation) is the development and refinement of your sensitivities with regard to your intuitive impulses.

Your highest potential, your True Wealth, has a greater opportunity for establishing itself when you make the commitment to raise your consciousness from a lower human order to living from *soul values* while serving your soul's purpose. And what are your soul's values? Vision, intelligence, integrity, love, humor, beauty, patience, the act of seeking heart connection, the urge to create, the urge to nurture while releasing the urge to alienate—to name a few.

Imagine for a moment there is a new education model and you volunteer at a school that embodies it because you love the *cause* (a new, as-yet-untried education model that embraces those kids that have, in the past, fallen through the cracks). Your experience is deeply gratifying to you because you are giving service, with passion and love, while contributing to the materialization of a vision. You feel joy in the fact that you are part of the *cause* of a new education model. When you heal the past while fulfilling soul intention, you find at some point that you are living from cause: just like in the school example; just like I did while working privately with clients. What is it like to live from cause? Life becomes ever new. With passion and vision, you experience a vibrant life of continuously expanding potential. Live from *cause*, and you are creating *daily* within the process a new, higher life experience—either the mastery of a talent or the happy resolution of a challenged area of life. What's more, you are highly aware of Life's (Spirit's) *daily* support.

Fulfilling soul intention, then, is a creative process. To consciously live the creating process requires a strong relationship between your inner responses to life's situations and your outer creative actions.

Take a moment to think about the familiar steps in the creative process:

Step 1. You have a vision in the form of an idea.
Step 2. You develop the idea and create a plan.
Step 3. You take outside action to build a series of positive results, one at a time.
Step 4. The original plan is materialized. (Interestingly, when you think back on the road to success, it's hard to see how it unfolded.)

Far too often, people who want to engage in a creative endeavor find themselves at the beginning of Step Three (taking outside action) and quit. The reasons?

- Doubt has set in.
- They are too fearful.
- They see the responsibility they will have to carry, and they don't want it.
- It is hard for them to accept the beauty and the power of who they will become.
- There is a strong belief that they don't deserve success.
- A part of them simply cannot believe success will ever happen.

These reasons constitute resistances. No judgment here. It is all right not to be ready, and resistance is perfectly understandable. The truth is that when you set out to live your purpose daily with committed fearlessness, your life will change in a number of ways while you're in process. You experience an acceleration of Spirit moving to support you. Spirit supplies events that are generally subtle, especially in the beginning. There are times, however, when they're not so subtle. In fact, they are clear and detailed, and you witness Life's forces purifying your past *daily*!

Among the effects you may notice are these:

- A great feeling of being in the right place at the right time.
- People with particular expertise or knowledge that you need to move yourself along make themselves known to you in synchronistic ways.
- You find a great new clarity and new meaning with regard to your reasons for doing what you are doing, and new learning's occur as a result of your efforts.
- You are in a better position to hear inner communications from your soul.
- Through conscious action toward soul fulfillment, the rest of the areas of your life are raised up. (A rising tide raises all boats.)

- Negative thoughts and fear-based feelings—such as anxiety, feeling adrift, being lost without purpose—stop controlling your thoughts and behavior, because you are living from the "light" of conscious observation.
- You experience more joy, more energy, and, often, a sense of timelessness.
- There is less fighting, less argument with, or resisting of life. Instead, there is the experience of being in greater harmony with life.
- As you near the goal of living more from Soul, there is a natural monetary wealth created by a balanced harmony with life and your passion—and there is simultaneously a passion to serve others in deep, meaningful ways from your natural talent.

All in all, when you live your purpose daily, you become a magnet. The Good in life is drawn toward you because you have become so much of what Good is within yourself. I would like to say that fear is no longer a part of your life experience, but the truth is that you will often face fear as you direct your actions toward success. Fear is simply a part of the process. The good news is that through fear, your courage muscle gets stronger. In a natural way, your appetite for spirit grows, drawing to you greater and higher experiences both in synchronistic events and inner "knowings." There comes a time when you can declare honestly, "I am spiritualizing from within."

When you are in alignment with your soul's reason for life and the "living process," you are in your *power zone*. It's like being inside a high-voltage wire that's connected back to the power plant. You can't see the force, but you can feel when you are in it. (I love the high this brings. I'm always left wanting more.)

THE UNSEEN HELPING HAND

The universe helps you by supporting your living processes in an infinite number of ways. Spirit can design exactly the right situations that are needed for your evolution and growth. It places you in situations that bring inner tensions to the surface—and in situations that heal your tensions, sometimes powerfully and instantaneously. It reveals, experientially, new understanding and information about who you are as well as newly discovered truths about life.

Life's natural orchestrated rhythms assigned to your soul's evolution can also place you in situations created to mirror from the outside something you are carrying inside (like when people asked me rapid-fire, anxious questions at my new job). It can also place you in situations that deliver confirming information about something you recently learned or already knew but didn't know you knew. And it can place you in situations that show you something profound about yourself, perhaps unearthing something in the subconscious that's held back Life's Flow for far too many years. With each healing, you spiritualize within. You are letting go of the subconscious habit of creating from the lower-personality self as you rise up to live more from your Soul Nature.

Spirit is so boundlessly creative and resourceful that it can arrange repeated messages because you didn't really get the learning the first time. (Often, the repeating is from a slightly different angle, which brings a deeper understanding of the Truth of what was just learned—but whenever and however life repeats, it's time to reconsider what It's trying to tell you.)

As you pay more attention to Spirit, you will notice it revealing things like:

- a new direction that will result in needed learning
- a new physical locale that is calling out to you
- prompts to do something you need to accomplish
- information about something you should *not* pursue
- information that you will require later

Spirit does not always pave an easy path. You can be placed in life circumstances that humble the ego (ugh!). You can be placed in situations that are a test to your readiness to move on. And you can be placed in situations that expose character flaws that weaken your integrity (for example, excessive jealousy or the habit of breaking promises to loved ones or even to yourself). But rest assured that although the path can be challenging, it is exactly the path you need.

CHALLENGES ALONG THE WAY

Let's take a close look at the more challenging nature of processing—the part where process has brought to the surface some inner subconscious belief that stands in your way of success and needs to be healed. The great indicator of such a situation is that something has happened to make you *react with emotion*, especially a *lot of negative emotion.* It can start when you are talking to someone and reactive negative emotions (anger, anxiety, fear) flare up. Your subconscious may believe you are talking to someone from your past (as mine did when I spoke to the mechanic at the muffler shop). Or a conversation may simply trigger a negative past experience, generating a deep sadness about something that you heard or witnessed long ago. Whatever it is, something was said or something happened, and now you are angry (*furious* might be a better word) or experiencing feelings of deep sadness. This is a place that needs healing—meaning that you have to let go of the dramas of the past to the point that you don't care about them anymore.

The key to processing the negative energies holding you earthbound is to do it as gracefully as possible. So let's look at a few things to remember when you are experiencing negative, reactive tension while processing:

1. Acknowledge! Acknowledge! Acknowledge! People who cannot firmly acknowledge that they are not feeling good about something or are in pain are avoiding the pain by pushing it away. There is a part of them that doesn't want to face an issue on a deep level. Some people are not ready to resolve the issue at hand. In fact, their egos continue to take pleasure in the drama.

2. Allow and observe! Have the courage to acknowledge the discomfort of the process. Now you are in a position to allow your lower self what it needs: time—time to openly feel, with your *acceptance*, negative feelings and complaints that are part of the problem.

3. Remain focused as the self-aware *observer*, or High Self. The conscious observer is actually light. It shines light (new information) onto the part of your subconscious that is healing. Stay calm and give your lower self the consideration it needs. As you do, the energy held in the subconscious around this particular life situation relaxes and so dissipates, making room for Spirit to enter. (When someone is talking to you with an agitated voice and your mind is asking, "Why is this person telling me this?" or, "Why is this person acting this way?" they are mirroring something that is activated within you. If your conscious *observer* can recognize this as it is happening, that is when you are using the mind as a tool for healing—aka reducing—the negative energies of your reactive self.)

4. Take responsibility for your "stuff." Own your contribution to a situation that has brought about your negative response. Do everything you can not to "dump on" (talk at) other people about the problem. Especially, do not engage negatively with the person (or persons) who is part of the tension. It's not their fault—at least not totally. Others have simply triggered what's going on inside you. Doing so only adds to (or feeds) the negative images of the past held in experiential memory.

   The goal is to diminish the negative energy, not increase it. Do everything you can not to act out of the reacting mind. Do everything you can not to feed the energy. Talking about it feeds the energy around the issue. Instead, "sit" calmly, observing how you are feeling, and be a witness as the negative sensations diminish, no matter how long it takes. When you do, space is created within yourself. That space is filled with the highest Spirit of what you are.

5. Keep a journal so you can pay close attention to life's orchestrated events and your rhythms and styles of processing.

6. Remember, reactive *drama is the enemy*! It adds to the negative energies held inside, reinforcing your view of life that sees everything from the lens of division ("if they win, I lose"). Drama creates the

need to control—to lust for the power to manipulate—and fosters alienation, when connection is actually the goal.

7. Seek the direction needed by observing from the inside, listening inside and outside to "see" the guiding events that navigate you through and into the wisdom of what the problem was all about in the first place.

8. Don't chase after situations that cause you to react. Let life bring them to you. Your role in Life's play is to pay minute-to-minute attention. *How am I feeling? What am I thinking?* Be glad when all is positive and cautious when it's negative. Observe, observe, observe!

9. Watch for the day when you become so used to not reacting that you find yourself embracing the tension when it happens, with gratitude, because you know when it is over that one more small piece of *who you really are* has been revealed.

10. It's really helpful if you can remember a time of great strength when you really lived from the *strength of who you were* (just as I remembered my strength while at the stove for the guru).

11. Turn to your spiritual practices to help you through. Relief from the ills of processing is one of the reasons to do yoga. So attend your favorite yoga class often. Repeat your favorite, most effective mantra all day long if needed. Countless times, words of a higher thought stream have saved me, shortening the duration of my discomfort. And, of course, meditate. Meditation at the third-eye center is very powerful and necessary for some of the intensities of processing that you may encounter. Try, if possible, to increase your meditation, either by adding more time to your normal practice session or adding another hour during the day. It is the number-one tool for developing the observer, which *is* the conscious self.

12. Nurture yourself. Make a list of things you love doing that nurture you. Then choose one thing from the list and do it. It is the lower self that is in pain. It is the lower self that, just like a small child, responds to being nurtured.

13. Refer to your images of an ideal future. These are the images you hold within of who you will be and the amazing life you will be living after dropping away the lower personality's thoughts of what life should be (the "it's all about me" thinking). Hold on to your vision of that future until the feelings of joy and good energy return once again.

14. Some techniques for processing take work; some not so much. Just remember that the key to (and the goal of) successful processing is to learn to participate as gracefully as possible.

15. Remember, processing is always temporary! Try to look at processing your negatives as the benefits of your good efforts, remembering always that because of the inner-purification process, you are spiritualizing within.

Let's take a break from all this instruction. In the next chapter, I'd like to tell you the story of the importance of commitment. Commitment happens with different levels of intensity. Each higher level deepens the meaning and purpose for doing what you are doing. The following chapter details a Life-orchestrated event designed to deepen and heighten my reason for working at Walt Baptiste's Hungry Mouth restaurant. I hope you enjoy it.

7

Wholehearted

After a little over three and a half years of working at the Hungry Mouth, I noticed a problem developing within myself. I was divided by a persistent voice of doubt—doubting just how long I could continue working there at the same pace. As a result, my love and passion regarding my reason for being there felt compromised. Truthfully, I felt so divided that I was in a state of torment. Walking away was completely out of the question. I loved creating food while reaching for higher and higher levels of quality with every dish. I loved being a part of Walt Baptiste's service to the public. Knowing that repeating mantra is a great antidote for troubled thoughts and feelings, I spent many hours repeating the guru's charged words—but even that didn't help.

On occasion, a customer would come into the kitchen to sit on a stool at the end of my workspace to chat and watch me work. I worked alone, so I considered these customers welcome guests. One told me about this small, old Asian movie theater in Chinatown. It showed movies produced in China and subtitled in English. "You've got to go there and watch this movie," he kept repeating. "You're going to love it. It's about Shaolin Kung Fu, an ancient form of martial arts." I think he repeated at least three times, "Do yourself a favor and go see that movie."

"OK, I got the message," I said. So on my next day off, after a plate of my favorite ginger beef with black-bean sauce and greens over rice, I settled into an old, dusty theater just in time to watch the opening credits.

THE COOK'S TALE

Back then, there were a lot of low-budget martial-arts movies produced in the central area of China. The filmmakers didn't have access to special-effects technology, so they instead hired actors that were at the top of their ability as martial artists. The directors would put them in front of the camera, turn it on, and yell, "Action!" The results were truly beautiful to watch: two or more young men authentically battling each other using amazing feats of speed and strength.

This particular film, the title of which I forgot long ago, took place in a small rural town in ancient China. It was during a period when roaming bands of thieves, knowing there were no armies or police forces to stop them, would raid small villages to steal its food supplies, along with its young women and anything else of value. Out of necessity, each village sent groups of its young men to the most famous training camps of Shaolin masters. When these men returned to their villages, they taught the remaining male residents, thus building their own protective army. Year after year, the tradition endured: every spring, the village elders sent ten to fifteen of their most talented young men to train with a Shaolin master.

The movie began with a group of elders announcing the names of their village's ten most talented teenage candidates, each to excited applause. In the next scene, the villagers lined the road to cheer and wish the young men well as they marched out of town, beginning their five-day walk to a Shaolin temple situated on a high plateau at the base of a majestic mountain.

Once they were clear of the villagers, the boys demonstrated their competitive nature by each claiming to have received the loudest applause. But one boy, Ju-Long, declined to join in the good-natured teasing. Everyone knew he was the most powerful and the cleverest among them and therefore the most favored by the villagers.

The temple compound was huge and held large buildings that could house two hundred and fifty students, the training staff, and the master himself. It included an expansive courtyard where students practiced their various forms of martial arts outdoors. There was also an outdoor arena with stadium-style seating. The compound was surrounded by twenty-five-foot walls designed to keep passersby from seeing in. In the center of one of the walls was a single small, wooden door just large enough to allow one person at a time to pass through.

As the boys approached, they knocked on the door. There was no answer, so they knocked again—louder this time—when suddenly, a peephole in the center of the door slid open. A voice yelled out, "What do you want?"

The boys replied, "We want to learn from the master."

The gatekeeper instructed the boys to line up single file. The door opened, and they began going in, one at a time. The eighth boy entered, the ninth boy entered. But when the tenth boy, Ju-Long, approached, the gatekeeper planted the open palm of his hand firmly into the center of the boy's chest, knocking him back, and said, "*Not you!*" Then he slammed the door in Ju-Long's face. The boy was crushed. He couldn't believe he had been barred for no apparent reason. He dropped to the ground, making an internal vow: "I am *not* leaving!"

There was no way the young man could go back to the village, and there was no way he could even bear to think of all his friends practicing something that was so close to his own heart while he could not. So Ju-Long had vowed to stay there, no matter how long it took to gain entry. Rain and shine, day and night, he stayed there. It was uncomfortably hot during the day, and the cold at night made it hard to sleep. After about a week, a small parcel was thrown over the fence to him: a rolled-up piece of cloth with a ball of rice inside. So he had some food, and he found a little stream nearby where he could drink water—surviving while remaining steadfast to his vow not to leave, no matter what!

On the thirtieth day, just as the sun began to reveal itself on the horizon, the door to the compound flew open. The gatekeeper stood silently holding the door wide so Ju-Long could enter. As he did, Ju-Long refused to let the gatekeeper see that his body had been shaking violently from the cold.

Inside was the courtyard where all the young men were practicing martial arts, with the master leading the practice. Ju-Long's heart leaped when he saw his friends from the village following the instructions of the master. But when he started walking toward them, the gatekeeper stopped him once again. "Not yet," he said. "Follow me."

The gatekeeper took Ju-Long into a room where a large amount of rice was cooked for three hundred hungry people three times a day: breakfast, lunch, and dinner. The room was very, very big, with a high ceiling. There was a large opening cut in the ceiling to allow cooking smoke to vent. In the very center of the room was a gigantic, wide stone table—longer than the average table by at least eight feet. In the stone tabletop were eight holes down the left side and eight holes down the right. The holes were just large enough for an oversized wok to sit in each one. And underneath the holes was another shelf made of stone. The shelf was where fires were set to cook the rice. All the woks were set up, with fires underneath attended to by kitchen workers who had just added water to the rice in each of the sixteen woks.

Wordlessly, the gatekeeper indicated with his bamboo rod that Ju-Long should stand in the center of the stone table, in between the two rows of woks. The gatekeeper handed the boy a long shaft made of solid wood that was slightly shorter than Ju-Long himself. "Use this to stir the rice as the water boils. And *don't let the rice burn,*" the gatekeeper said firmly.

When the water began to boil in wok after wok, Ju-Long, standing at one end of the table, began stirring. As more woks began to boil, Ju-Long's stirring action became more frantic. Startled by a loud *crack*, Ju-Long turned to see the gatekeeper at the opposite end of the table, banging the tabletop with his bamboo rod and saying, "These are starting to burn!" Ju-Long raced to the opposite end of the table and began stirring the rice in those woks. *Crack* came the sound again. "What about *these* woks?" yelled the gatekeeper. And so it went for a full hour, with Ju-Long running back and forth faster and faster as he moved his stirring pole more and more frantically to keep all the rice from burning.

When the rice was done, the kitchen workers emptied the cooked rice into holding containers, replacing each wok with a new one filled with uncooked rice and water, repeating the process over again. When the young boys from Ju-Long's village filed in for their morning meal, there was plenty of finger-pointing and jovial laughter at Ju-Long's turn of fate at becoming a lowly kitchen hand.

The following weeks turned into months. Each day, Ju-Long was the first one to enter and the last to leave the kitchen, while the others slept. The greatest challenge for him was staying aware of the two rows of rice-filled woks. As he turned to focus on the row to the right, he'd forget the row to the left (behind) him. It wasn't long before Ju-Long began to wonder if the gatekeeper could read his mind. It seemed that the moment he forgot the row of woks behind him, he'd hear the *crack* of the bamboo rod reminding him to be aware of what was both in front of him *and* behind him. In time, Ju-Long understood that he needed to be conscious of what was happening in all sixteen woks at the same time. He knew he had mastered that task the day the gatekeeper left the room, leaving him alone with his work.

The path to Ju-Long's sleeping quarters led him past the master's house each night. The house had a large window with a shoji-type screen through which the young man could see light and shadow. As the master practiced his Kung Fu moves, their shadows showed on the window screen. At first, Ju-Long was simply entranced by the master's moves: their speed, their power, their precision, their execution with grace and ease. But one night, Ju-Long couldn't contain himself. He began mirroring the master's movements. He began doing this every night until the master's light went out. Many nights, Ju-Long continued practicing the master's moves well into the small hours.

More months passed, and Ju-Long found his rhythm in the kitchen. To the outside observer, it looked as though he was dancing as he prepared the rice. Moving easily with lightning speed up and down the center aisle—stirring right, then stirring left—Ju-Long believed he had mastered his assignment and longed to join the young men in their daily practices.

One day, his village friends came to say good-bye. Their training was over, and they were heading home. It was clear that Ju-Long was saddened by their departure and longed to leave with them, but he couldn't, because his training wasn't over. The next week, another group of boys from his village came for training. Ju-Long's hesitancy to speak openly with the new group made it increasingly obvious how much he yearned to return home. Ju-Long's longing led to moments of pleasant daydreams of his youthful village life. His mixed emotions and daydreaming became such distractions that the rice was all too often left to burn in one or two of the woks.

Any thoughts of mastery were suddenly cut short when the gatekeeper made his presence known once again. Ju-Long hadn't seen him enter the room since he was deep in his subconscious thoughts of home. That changed when he felt a sharp pain across his back. "*Wake up!*" the gatekeeper yelled. More training! Ju-Long was now more positive than ever that the gatekeeper knew what he was thinking, because the moment he let his mind drift into a daydream, he would feel a sharp slap across his back. "*Wake up!*" the gatekeeper would yell again. "*No more dreams!*"

This phase of Ju-Long's training went on for several more months. One afternoon, the gatekeeper left the kitchen briefly to return with a long rope. Without a word, he had one of the kitchen workers secure one end of the rope to a beam high above the center of the stone table. He wrapped the other end around Ju-Long's waist, tying it in place at the base of his back. "This will make it easier for you to keep the rice from burning," the gatekeeper explained. "By swinging on the rope, you'll be able to move quickly from one end of the table to the other."

So, using the rope for support, Ju-Long created a series of moves designed to propel him from one wok to another. One of his favorites was to kick his legs out and around, making a wide arc as he swung with a single movement from one end of the table to the other. He also created arcs of varying lengths to plant his stirring pole with amazing speed and accuracy, not allowing even one wok of cooking rice to burn and not splashing a single drop of water. His unique antics and his speed and accuracy with the stirring pole moved the other kitchen workers to admiration, even awe. This phase, too, went on for many months.

One afternoon, the gatekeeper entered the kitchen and, as he untied Ju-Long's rope, announced, "That's enough. We're going to put someone else in your place." Ju-long followed the gatekeeper into the arena, and there, sitting in the stadium seats, were all two hundred and fifty of the school's students. In the first row, at center, was the master himself. In an atmosphere of calm silence, Ju-Long walked to the middle of the arena with his wok-stirring pole and faced the master, thinking he was about to announce something. Instead, a long, still silence ensued. Then a student from the group of onlookers stood up. He had a pole of about the same length and thickness as Ju-Long's. With a fierce scream and lightning speed, the student attacked our hero. In his confusion, Ju-Long discovered that he could match, move for move, his challenger's threatening advances. Instinctively, he had accessed the reactive, defensive moves he had learned while keeping the rice from burning.

As the challenge continued, Ju-Long quickly realized that he knew what to do naturally and that he was not afraid of his challenger. One of the moves Ju-Long used to confuse his opponent was to leap with a swinging motion, his legs landing to the left or right of the challenger, just as if he were still tied to his rope. One instant, he was facing his opponent, the next he was at his left or right—which provided opportunities for Ju-Long to strike hard with his pole. After a few minutes, when it was clear that Ju-Long was the better fighter, the master raised his hand, signaling the two boys to stop.

In the next instant, Ju-Long was attacked by four more young men, each also armed with a wooden pole. But fighting off four attackers felt easier to him than keeping sixteen woks of boiling rice from burning. After Ju-Long issued dozens of consecutive bruising blows to his challengers, the master raised his hand again, indicating that the challenge was over. From the smile on his face, everyone knew Ju-Long was enjoying himself.

During the challenges, there was a man sitting to the right of the master. Ju-Long understood him to be the master's most advanced instructor. The instructor, who did not have a pole, bowed in respect to the master and then approached Ju-Long, preparing to challenge him. After the instructor took a few deep breaths and made a few preparatory Kung Fu movements with his body, the fight began.

The first move the instructor made was to slap Ju-Long's pole hard with a downward motion while at the same moment jumping high and landing full force onto the middle of the pole, breaking it in half. In the next moment, the instructor executed a sweeping, 360-degree kick, knocking the remaining section of the pole out of Ju-Long's hands. And in the next moment, the instructor struck Ju-Long in the chest with five powerful blows, nearly knocking him over. But Ju-Long's moves, the result of his late-night shadow training, took over as he met his challenger blow for blow.

Because of both men's determination, it was clear to everyone in the arena that this was a battle to the end. When the instructor lay bloodied and near unconscious on the ground, ending the longest, most intense challenge to Ju-Long's abilities, the master rose—as did everyone in the stadium—and bowed to Ju-Long. The master, smiling with admiration, moved close to Ju-Long's ear and, speaking softly, said to him, "Now you can go home."

MESSAGE RECEIVED

The reason I share this story and it's transforming results with you is that, on occasion, a message is not delivered in small, subtle pieces. A message can, in fact, show up with amazing clarity and directness. It can convey a realization with perfect timing, when the impact of it transforms your understanding about who you are and what you are born to do, or it offers the resolution to a long-held, seemingly hopeless dilemma, or simply a Truth about Life. At the same time, such a message can impart the understanding that you are being taken care of, that your questions are heard and your struggles observed—and that your needs can be met directly. In all of these ways, this movie changed everything for me.

When it ended and I stood up, I felt that a great change had come over me. I returned to the Hungry Mouth restaurant the next day and never again entertained doubts about what I was doing or why I was doing it. Because *now* my reason for being there contained a deeply felt level of meaning and *personal* purpose…greater than it ever had before. A new, expanded vision supplemented my wholehearted actions. And *no one* (including myself) could ever persuade me to change direction.

In the next chapter, we'll discover the deeper reasons that Walt Baptiste established the four disciplines as a foundation for soul fulfillment and spiritual growth, and the potential results from their steady application.

8

A Deeper Look / A Call to Adventure

I love it when I start reading a book, thinking that the contents will be interesting—and wind up elated when it turns out to be so inspiring that I'm disappointed when it ends. That said, all too many people believe that spiritual growth comes from books. The answers to spiritual inquiry cannot be found in books. Books, including this one, can be excellent tools for gaining insights into one's particular life at the right moment and into life in general. But the most one can hope for from a book is inspiration (albeit that at the right time, the right book or right passage in a book can provide a deep healing or a life-changing inspiration).

The confusion lies in the commonly accepted definition of spiritual growth. Google the phrase, and you find "learning about and expanding in your understanding of things spiritual." I'm sure there is some merit to that definition, but what it describes has not been my experience. Spiritual growth, in my personal opinion, is brought about by raising our rate of energy as beings closer to and in harmony with a union with God—who is a Spirit. To my knowledge, this happens only one way: through experiences.

The purpose of this book is, of course, to inform its readers. My deeper hope for it is that it be a source of inspiration, inspiring you to such a degree that you will willingly open the door to an entirely new, expanded reason for living by embracing a higher life path—one that includes seeking a very personal spiritual experience while simultaneously fulfilling your soul's desire for mastery in one of life's arenas. In fact, I hope you begin your consciousness-expanding path with such deeply felt commitment that you wouldn't dream of returning to a life focused solely on material pursuits. Needless to say, these are the results I would love every reader to experience, but in reality, I know that different people respond differently to information.

Walt Baptiste made it very clear to his students that the responsibility for committed action is left completely up to the individual. His health and spiritual guidance gave people the resources to learn and build each foundational pillar, and Walt emphasized the need for each activity in his classes. But there was no insisting, no scheduling when something had to be completed, no exams to pass. Yes, his Center included a yoga and meditation room, a gym, a health-food store, and a health-food restaurant, but cultivating a high level of proficiency in each foundational discipline was entirely up to us. Our test as his students was in our determination to find our personal rhythms for establishing each principle as a way of life.

Obviously, the responsibility for further action is up to you. It is no secret that human nature pretty much guarantees that most people delay starting any new self- improvement discipline, sometimes even for as long as a few years. It is even more typical that people engage with one for a few months and then stop. There are also people who work hard to engage in all five principles for a year or two but then also stop. The human condition is complicated, so there are a lot of different reasons for discontinuing something that brings beauty and happiness into our lives. I believe that one of the reasons is that most people never have a clear understanding of the original purposes for meditation and yoga practice. To help bring you to a more committed level of sustained action, I think it would be helpful to describe in more detail the reasons for and potential outcomes of each of the principles of Walt Baptiste's form.

PASSION

Before beginning any action toward soul realization and spiritual growth, there must be either an ongoing desire for a very personal spiritual experience or a great yearning to fulfill your soul's needs for this lifetime.

I once heard the testimony of a young woman who was unhappy but didn't know why. At one time, she liked her job, enjoyed the company of a few close friends, and had no trouble dating. Now, even though none of the conditions had changed, her life was tainted with a somber sadness. More and more, she withdrew from friends and loved ones, choosing instead to spend long hours alone at home. One Sunday morning, she was pacing around her bedroom when, for no apparent reason, she had the thought, *If only I could feel God's Love*. And *she did*! In the subsequent moments, her heart turned on, and the light in the room brightened. "Blissful joy" was the phrase she used to describe the experience.

After that experience, her life turned beautiful once again, now infused with an ongoing, deep, heartfelt, unyielding passion to once again experience God's Love. Her wisdom told her that deep, life-changing, spiritual experiences are not created; they are blessings. They are blessings that "just happen." So she focused her passion on finding ways to open up to more spiritual possibilities. Following her instincts, she developed what she found was *her* meditation technique. It was desire that had brought the first experience, so her meditation started with the repeating of her desire for Spirit to enter her once again, followed by a focused, open silence to allow Spirit to enter.

As time passed, she experienced the Love of Spirit so often that people began asking her how they too could experience Spirit firsthand. The more she shared her experiences, the more she realized she had become a servant to a higher calling: a woman with a mission for defining the ways that people could set an intention for a spiritual experience. Happiness ensued as she fulfilled her soul's desire to serve the God that she knew resided in everyone who asked her help.

So, first comes the desire for a spiritual experience: an acknowledgment by Spirit that inspires and redirects one's life toward the requirements for developing a closer relationship with God. Alternatively, there may be a burning desire to direct one's soul-driven actions toward the fulfillment of the soul's mission during this life cycle.

THE NATURE OF THE SOUL

Each day that the world gives us should be finding our efforts more and more as devotees of Soul-Life.

—*WALT BAPTISTE*

Not everyone has one of those door-opening, life-transforming spiritual experiences. But if your desire is to serve a higher calling, what's the best way to ensure you will do so? Uncover your soul's vision for an ideal life experience and direct your life toward its fulfillment.

This is good, practical advice for a lot of reasons, one of the biggest being that your soul's number-one desire is its reason for participating in the human drama in the first place—and the ultimate aim of that drama is to move closer to God. Your soul's ultimate desire and goal is a perfect union with all that God Is. To move one step closer to its desire, your soul needs the experience of living through the resolution of your life's purpose. It needs the vitality that is gained through the struggle of mastering a life challenge or talent. It needs that specific vitality and experiential knowledge to bring alive the part of the soul that is keeping it from a union with Spirit. Your soul needs a particular life experience because having that experience will result in lifting its rate of vibration closer to a Divine Union. (Spirit's rate of vibration is at such a high frequency that if we were to suddenly vibrate at it, the body's nervous system would burn out just as a light bulb does when charged with too much voltage. That is why evolution is a one-step-at-a time process. More about this later.)

Your soul has its mission for this life experience. It lies in the area of soul-evolving experiences that will raise its rate of vibration, expand its intelligence, its wisdom, and its ability to love toward the same omniscience, omnipotence, and universal benevolence that God is. Your soul and its etheric body are immortal, so whatever constructive efforts you make toward fulfillment—whether successful or not—become part of the soul's evolution and remain after the material body dies.

The following are a few more thoughts to consider about the soul:

- Your soul's evolutionary process is like an iceberg—in that most of it exists below the surface. Of the process, 5 percent or less is witnessed at the conscious level, while 95 percent takes place on the subconscious level. Engaging in Walt Baptiste's foundational form for soul and spiritual growth raises the process more and more to the conscious level while it accelerates your soul's evolution.
- Your soul evolves simultaneously as you mature emotionally and psychologically through the successes and failures in your life.
- As you make efforts toward mastering one of your soul's intentions, there comes a point when your efforts naturally serve others. The closer to mastery, the greater the service. Your energy levels rise to such a point that when in the presence of others, the mere state of your being benefits those others without words.
- Your soul is an integral part of who you are. But just as your emotional body is different from your physical body, your soul, with its immortal, astral body, is different from your material body.
- Unless it is your particular calling, the soul normally is not interested in saving the outside world but rather in mastering its reason for being here. The soul knows that when it does this, you will enjoy the ease and joy of being aligned and in harmony with Life Itself.
- Aside from Spirit, your soul is your most powerful creative energy force. As a result, living from the energy of soul brings to the body an unusually high—some may even say an uncommon—level of energy, happiness, and health.
- Your soul's nature is grounded in love. Its response to life is to reach out, to embrace rather than divide and withdraw. Your soul seeks to nurture the well-being of your family and your loved ones as well as the people in its sphere of influence.
- The soul is your conscience, *your* moral compass pointing to the rightness or wrongness of *your* life. A close monitoring of the soul's

communications will naturally create a moral decisiveness for the benefit of your life as well as the lives of your loved ones.

Just how does your soul communicate to you? Your soul is obligated to allow the freedoms of your personality's choices to be expressed in all decisions of the lower life. If your life choices are negative, resulting from habits of hurting yourself and others, the soul tends to withdraw any communication. But if your intentions aim toward expressing the higher human qualities within yourself while respecting the same qualities in others, your soul draws closer.

Of course, your soul doesn't announce to your lower mind, "This is an idea from your soul." In fact, your soul doesn't communicate to you directly. It communicates with a steady stream of reminder thoughts that create a desire to do something specific. For years, long before Walt Baptiste opened the Hungry Mouth, whenever I ate in a restaurant, I would observe the experience and create a scenario in my mind of how I would manage it if I owned it: which people I would want working for me and which I would replace; changes I'd make to the menu; how I would redesign the dining room, and so on. And my mind would continue creating the ideal restaurant long after leaving. Spiritual masters know your soul's needs, so, hearing my soul's yearning for a restaurant- creating experience, Walt Baptiste asked me to help him build and manage his restaurants.

Your soul's most obvious communication is through emotion, a passionate urge pointing you in a specific direction. An example might be that of a ten-year-old boy attending a concert featuring a classical guitarist and becoming filled with a burning passion to play with the skill of the master he just witnessed. This represents an experience of the soul's area of genius needing to be expressed.

Your soul also understands karma, the law of cause and effect. It understands that the requirement for creating more freely in your life is the purification of all past karmic debt and emotional wounding. It also knows that the best antidote for karmic debt is service to others. It yearns for the freedoms of full expression that you will have once you live from your soul and all that holds you earthbound is surrendered.

I didn't start working at the stove with a passion for cooking. In fact, I didn't really know why Walt Baptiste put me there. What I did know is that he had the ability to give people the work that most suited who they were. So I began thinking that the deeper reason would make itself known with time. At the end of the first year, it was clear that (sometimes) the food I made helped people to feel better. There was a possibility that they would bring friends and someone, sooner or later, would venture into one of Walt Baptiste's classes. Now there was passion. I had a reason for creating every dish, every time better than the last, while I was serving a higher cause for the guru. The gift I received for serving his mission for fifteen years was the burning away of massive amounts of my karmic debt.

There are signs of your purpose. Pay attention to your urges and, even more, learn to follow them. Whatever you are drawn to, do *with a persistent desire*. Follow through and do it. If it's really a desire of the ego, you'll know soon enough. A soul urge could easily be a passion to do something that you have pushed aside for years, but the thought of it and the passion for doing it won't leave you alone. Is there a consistent thread, a theme to your life that has always been there, even just in the background? Throughout my life, mine has always been a deep desire to learn everything I can about the nature of human nature.

I once heard a great story about a man who followed through with the things he liked to do. In 1935, this particular man, Joe, while working in a nearby city for a mechanic fixing cars, found that he had a knack for fixing car radios. The radios back then weren't built well enough to survive road vibrations, and the shop owner made sure he checked every one that came in, because their repair brought in new revenue. In fact, Joe enjoyed fixing radios so much that he found he preferred working on radios to repairing cars. Eventually, he opened a radio-repair shop in his small hometown.

Joe was one of those people who liked chatting with his customers almost more than he liked fixing their radios, so it wasn't long before his business was a thriving success. Joe also found he enjoyed listening to music while he fixed radios, and soon, a lot of his customers were asking him about the music he played at the shop. So Joe added an inventory of record albums to it. As time passed, Joe's record section earned more revenue than his radio repair, and he found more pleasure in talking to people about music than in repairing radios—so he stopped repairing radios, renamed his store, and sold records. He still kept a small inventory of new radios for sale.

Next, Joe found that he really had a fascination for classical music. His small Midwestern-town customers had never listened to classical music, choosing instead to buy the most popular albums. That didn't matter to Joe. He ordered both styles of music, popular and classical albums, which he played for his own pleasure. On occasion, a customer would ask him about the music. Joe would play for the customer the albums he or she liked the most, pointing out inspiring passages—and people began buying the classical albums. As his classical-music section and its buying public grew, Joe found that people shared his enjoyment for talking about the classics, so he cleared out the dusty old storeroom in back and built a place there for regular meetings. "Come Join Our Music Club," read the sign over the door to the back room.

Years passed. When Joe retired, there was a large contingent of people in his small town that listened to and enjoyed classical music, which never would have existed had it not been for Joe's talent for continually doing what he loved.

If you are having trouble finding greater meaning to your life, ask yourself if there is a common thread of interest throughout it that has always given you great pleasure.

MEDITATION

Meditation is the crowning practice for spiritual growth and should always remain your focus as the one practice that will bring you closer to the goal of spiritual advancement and the potential for spiritual experiences.

As I've mentioned, one of the most common breakdowns when attempting a new direction in life, especially when it involves a series of disciplines for self-discovery, is that people don't follow through. They stop shortly after starting. There are many reasons that this happens, but it so often boils down to people having no real understanding of the *inner* purposes of the yoga or meditation they are practicing. Their reasons for doing these things are not in alignment with the original purposes of the practices. For example, I sometimes ask people why they like yoga. They answer with things such as, "I like the way it makes me feel," or, "I know it's good for me, and I like doing something that is good for me," or, "I need to stay flexible." Recently, I have heard more people saying, "I want to discover why I was born," which is wonderful. But I have never heard, "I want to grow spiritually." Don't get me wrong: I know there *are* people who want to take advantage of yoga and meditation for their original spiritual-growth intentions. And many people love yoga for its many health and emotional benefits for the body. But even they often (although not always) stop for some misplaced reason.

Some good people start regular yoga and meditation classes because they are in the middle of a life crisis. For example, they have lost a sense of joy with life, or they are stuck in the confusion of a dilemma. For example, one woman came to meditation and yoga classes because she sensed her marriage was over but didn't have the courage to end it. Her hope was that the teacher would somehow resolve the problem, when in fact the teacher is there to set the stage for students to access the resolution to the problem that already resides within them. When this woman realized that she had to take full responsibility for leaving or staying in her marriage, she stopped coming to class.

As for meditation, part of why people have difficulties when learning to meditate is that many techniques and processes that are labeled as meditation are not. For example, some classes teach people how to creatively visualize a beautiful and safe environment, followed by instructions for looking for answers to a life issue or for programming life in a specific direction. The results may have great therapeutic effects for the mind and emotions, but even so, this is not meditation—it's a creative-visualization therapy. On the other hand, when people attend a class that teaches the actual principles of meditation, many of them are disappointed when they find it involves a lot more than an exercise for feeling better. In fact, in the beginning, the practice is a largely uncomfortable work for body, mind, and emotions that haven't been prepared for the requirements of an hour of real meditation. Many well-intentioned seekers have been disillusioned as a result of attaching the label of meditation to so many practices that are not meditation.

A Webster's dictionary definition for meditation includes this phrase: "to engage in contemplation or reflection." To me (please remember, these are just my opinions), contemplation and reflection are effective and helpful disciplines of the mind, but they are not meditation. Walt Baptiste on occasion would recommend we engage in the principles of introspection and retrospection, two very powerful principles of the mind for self-discovery, but he never identified them as meditation. Likewise, mental exercises for personal material gain, such as visualizing a favorable sum of money in the bank or focusing inner attention mentally on a person to uncover their motives or to find a solution to a conflict you are having with someone are great and worthy uses of the mind, but they are not meditation.

The next Webster's definition comes a lot closer: "to engage in mental exercise (as concentration on one's breathing or repetition of a mantra) for the purpose of reaching a heightened level of spiritual awareness." The following are a few words written by Walt Baptiste that will also help with the clarification and purpose for meditation practice:

The highest sacrifice we as individuals can attain is to master ourselves in Meditation, which is to liberate Consciousness from being prisoner of gross matter.

The fact is, Meditation is designed by Higher-Intelligence for the Spiritualization of the Consciousness. It is not intended originally to improve our material circumstances. It is truly meant to reveal and strengthen us within self in our capacities and personal power to be independent and free from the vicissitudes of gross material circumstances. All the tremendous help to our physical dilemma can only be a side effect and not the objective. In truth, HIGHER MIND, when gifting mankind the art, science, technique and Grace of Meditation, had no concern with the average man-made existence, as meditation was the opportunity to realize higher states of Being.

Spiritual practice evolves as we daily sincerely apply ourselves with all our heart. The devotional attitude, the doing of all works for God—these combined, will take care of the trinity of the physical-mental-spiritual development to its perfection in the Unconscious.

The irony is that with meditation, improvements in daily life arrive that are indications that your good efforts are a success. Noticing the many life-lifting experiences that are the evidences of an effective meditation practice; it isn't long before the mind slips into a desire for more. At the beginning of each meditation, try to form the habit of announcing your intention to Spirit that the purpose for your practice is to realize Spirit, or your desire to have spiritual experience. Forming the habit of announcing your intention helps to keep your mind aware of the original reason that meditation is so important to you.

Even without doing that, however, its wonderful benefits will become part of your life. When you hold your concentrated attention at the *ajna* center in the middle of the head, you bring increased amounts of energy to that center. (Where the mind is held, energy follows.) The energy that accumulates there is the life force, or vibrant spiritual essence. As a result of its accumulation, your higher human faculties are developed and refined, and your consciousness expands. In fact, all the subtle human capabilities—intuition, instincts, voices of higher guidance, psychic awareness, and so on—improve.

The witness aspect of your mind awakens more and more. There is a greater presence accompanying moment-to-moment life. Life choices resulting from mental clarity come from a greater level of maturity, intelligence, and wisdom. With greater wisdom, life smooth's out; its ups and downs are not so dramatic. Things that used to seem so important aren't anymore. In fact, you can't remember why they ever were.

One caveat: you may go through a period where memories from your past enter your mind over and over. To me, that is a really good sign. The memories are important to a particular phase of advancement you are passing through. It means you are letting go of your attachment to the old you and moving on to another stage in life.

YOGA

> *The body, when it is mastered in balance, harmony, unity and oneness is of the highest fitness for Meditation.*
>
> —*WALT BAPTISTE*

Yoga classes are not a new idea. There is evidence that yoga was practiced five thousand years ago and that the original purpose was for reducing the ego by gaining self-knowledge and wisdom through the postures. Today, there is a real mishmash of styles and teachers to choose from. There are yoga styles and also teachers that are labeled and touted as better than others, but to me, they are all beautiful additions to the mainstream of our culture—simply because regularly attending any yoga class is better than no yoga classes at all.

Among the many styles of yoga is Walt Baptiste's method, which I believe is a very close representation of the original intended approach to the yoga postures (again, just my opinion). I base my (prejudiced) opinion on the fact that the main focus of Walt Baptiste's style is an all-inclusive preparation of the student's physical, mental, and emotional bodies for meditation. He achieves it by continued reminders to students to stay conscious of what they are thinking, using the mind to direct the body and the emotions toward a deep letting go while in posture.

Walt Baptiste devised a pattern for breathing in harmony with the movement of the yoga postures. That, along with his continued reminders to think and feel in the moment, tended to calm the mind. One of the essential outcomes of his classes was a beautiful harmonizing of the three main bodies—physical, mental, and emotional—focusing them toward the ideal direction of a calm, peaceful inner surrender.

The following points describe many of the potential results of a steady regimen of yoga when practiced in the Walt Baptiste style *or any authentic yoga style*:

- Yoga postures strengthen the body, especially the back, making it easy to remain in a seated meditation posture for extended periods. Normally, the body and emotions hold levels of stress at varying degrees. A yoga class can be great therapy for the body and emotions by releasing, and deeply smoothing away, internal tensions.

- A regimen of yoga classes lowers the body's normal levels of tension. Imagine that there is a scale for the normal inner tension levels that are held by the average person: absolute tension to the highest extreme is at 100, and the lowest possible tension-free experience is at 0 (which represents the death of the body). Let's say that the normal reading of tension held by a healthy individual is 55. As an individual remains steady and sincere in his or her yoga practice, the tension held in the body lowers to, say, 30 or even 25. The lower the number, the greater the body's health and energy. The lowest levels of held tension also allow for greater success in meditation. In the beginning, seated meditation posture exposes great levels of tension in the body. As one nears the mastering of meditation, the seated body becomes relaxed, as if it were lying in bed, waiting for sleep.

- A steady stream of weekly yoga classes heightens self-awareness. Self-awareness is the main human characteristic needed for mastering the inner-purification process. Refined levels of observing inner emotional and mental responses to outside events facilitate more intelligent, mature choices.

- Heightened senses form a greater relationship with the subtler aspects of being human. Yoga practitioners will begin to relate more strongly to the *energies* of their bodies as levels of health and strength rise. Yoga classes encourage the core energies residing deep within to surface, integrating and invigorating the material body's cells.

- Yoga postures activate the primary energy centers, the chakras—especially the first chakra located at the base of the spine, which releases a strong flow of subtle life force up the spine and into the brain.
- Yoga expands both ends of your inner scale for experiences of deep calm with high levels of energy.

People who live from habits, recycling the same patterns at work, with family, and with friends will emotionally and psychologically form a narrow—and, hence, mediocre—relationship with life. Yoga opens, deepens, and widens your psychological and emotional capacities for experiencing an ever-expanding relationship with all aspects of life.

PHYSICAL FITNESS AND HEALTHY DIET

Even the body shall "know."

—*WALT BAPTISTE*

One of the most important things to understand about spiritual growth is the fact that growing spiritually means that the energy levels of your state of being in the physical body, the etheric body, and the soul will increase to a higher vibrating frequency. The increases happen incrementally through three main activities: steady attention to daily meditation, yoga postures, *and* a *serious* form of body conditioning. By serious, I mean a form of focused exercise that has a beginning (warm-up), a middle (increasing your heart rate to a target appropriate for your age for an extended period of time), and an end (cooldown). The easiest and best environment for developing the habit of building health is a nearby health club, YMCA, or similar facility.

External methods for body improvements must be utilized in combination with the internal methods of meditation. Meditation alone will not do for the body what the combination of inner and outer remedies will offer. The Goal of the Master Path for the body cannot be attained without the total practices that purify, heal, and regenerate within and outwardly. The physical and spiritual techniques must go hand in hand for the uncovering of the Soul.

—*WALT BAPTISTE*

When you are in meditation, your concentration is held at the forehead center. Here, spiritual essence builds, affecting the brain cells and the pineal and pituitary glands. Spiritual essence also moves down the spine, stimulating the movement of the energy in the heart and the full range of the chakra system. In turn, the energy levels of the cells throughout the entire body are raised. But here's the most important part: Spirit is infinitely intelligent and will only deliver the amount of energy your body can handle, and no more. But the goal of your yoga and meditation practices is to raise your state of being as high as possible before your time in this life runs out. The body that's conditioned can accept higher energy intensities and integrate them faster.

Every time you sit in meditation, you draw spiritual essence into yourself, lifting your state of being. Every time you heal an emotional wound, every time you surrender attachment to a false, conditioned belief and replace it with a higher truth, spiritual essence rushes in to lift your state of being one small step closer to God's. Go to the gym, and the new levels of energy are integrated and preserved in the body. Neglect the body's health, and what spiritual essence does enter dissipates.

For more than a year, after every monthly lunch I had with my fellow student and workout coach, Norman (I mentioned earlier that he began his study with Walt Baptiste in the late 1950s and was his most advanced student), his good-bye was a firmly stated, "Stay in shape!" I thought he was simply reminding me to remain steady with my workouts, which didn't make a lot of sense. He knew I rarely missed a workout. But soon enough, I understood.

During a conversation with a close friend, he happened to say something that triggered a realization that released a massive amount of fear-based, negative energy I had taken on when I was eleven. The original incident had occurred when I witnessed a debilitating event involving a friend my age, his father, and his mother. It pertained to what amounted to an age-old family-crisis story. The mother had disappeared with another man, and the boy's father fell apart emotionally. Because he couldn't leave the house, he lost his job. Our families were neighbors for years, so the boy and I had had many grand childhood adventures together. But when his mother left and I saw the devastating effect it had on him and his father, I felt a deep sympathy for their sorrow. In the midst of the father's angry rants about the evils of his wife and of all women, I did all I could as an eleven-year-old to help both father and son. In the process, I took on a huge, fear-filled energy cloud of suffering that included their anger and their pain in being abandoned. Years later, my friend's innocent comment caused me to realize that their pain actually had nothing to do with me. My induced fear of being the recipient of a woman's pain-inflicting abandonment was instantaneously surrendered, *and Spirit rushed in.*

How long did it take for me to integrate this new energy? Two weeks! It was the one and only time I missed a day of work because of the spiritual-growth process. My mind was calm, simply because it was impossible to think about anything other than reviewing and making reasoned sense of what had happened and the way I was feeling. I had an interesting level of overall energy, but physically, I was very weak. For the following two weeks, I had to take care to keep minimally involved with life.

"I told you to stay in shape," was Norman's first comment when I next saw him.

Now do you understand the importance of body conditioning for spiritual growth?

Diet and vitamin supplements play an important role when integrating higher levels of energy that result from your good efforts. One or maybe even two days after a particularly powerful transforming experience, you may notice that you are unusually hungry. If you are paying attention, you will know it's the body's need for calories to burn and of nutrients for rebuilding. It is a principle of the body, when rebuilding, to surpass its original levels of strength and health and become a little stronger, a little healthier than it was previously, just in case you are faced with the same transforming demands again. (The cells also require a steady supply of healthy, nutritious food, not just for integration but also for remaining balanced and grounded during the inner purification process.)

Two words of caution: be practical! The idea is to build a *strong foundation* of health and strength. Think about the construction of a building. A foundation is the unmoving base structure that supports the building above so that it stays level and balanced. Gym workouts, diet, and vitamin supplements designed for higher health of the body are the foundations for supporting balance during the inner-purification and spiritual-integration process.

When it comes to supplements, try to stay with a commonsense regimen. They are *supplements,* after all. Some people go off the deep end, experimenting with the latest fad diets or using large quantities of a particular vitamin because someone told them some sort of miracle would happen. Exercise full responsibility for your commonsense decisions. Yes, there are people who can prescribe a chemistry of healing through nutrition. If that is your calling, then take the same path they did and throw yourself into the education needed to be unusually effective in the realm of your health and nutrition interests.

Let your body tell you what it needs in the form of a healthy diet. Try to find the diet that is best suited to your body type. Most people need some form of meat protein. Then again, other bodies are much better suited to a light vegetarian diet with an occasional bit of meat. There might be a time when you find it is better to stop animal proteins and move toward a steady vegetarian diet for a year or two. Then, when the time is right, you find your inclination returns to a diet that includes meat. Let your body tell you how to achieve optimal, balanced health and strength, and keep your ego out of it.

The goal is to live the meaning of Walt Baptiste's words: "I am mastered in the balance, harmony, unity and oneness of the highest fitness for Meditation."

FREEDOM: MADE IN AMERICA

I often wondered why Walt Baptiste was born an American. He could have chosen any culture he wanted. Regrettably, I never asked him the question, so officially, I don't know the answer. But my instincts tell me he was here to introduce to our American culture a very practical system of soul discovery and spiritual growth that fits nicely into the rhythms of our everyday life. The timing for bringing his teachings to America and the world is also interesting. I believe that he brought his teachings to the world because they will play a major role in the current, very important unfolding period in human history.

He began his mission in the mid-1930s at the young age of seventeen, when he opened his first gym in the living room of his father's house. He left his material body on July 6, 2001, at age eighty-three, sixty-six days before the 9/11 attack on the World Trade Center that began a new era of worldwide uncertainty—an era in which paradigms of trusted life-supporting systems are breaking apart.

In my opinion, Walt Baptiste came when he did to give us the techniques we will need to take the best possible advantage of the powerful waves of change-inducing energies sweeping the world today. He chose to be American because the structure of our culture allows for and supports the creative freedoms to choose a higher life path. You don't have to go to a monastery or live in an ashram to evolve consciously or have spiritual experience. Instead, you are free to answer the call of your soul's reason for this life cycle; you can develop it, serve from it, and master it *while* growing spiritually into your authentic self, and our American culture will encourage you and support you.

Today, the urge to mediocrity has given way to the rhythms and challenges of change, both materially and internally. As a culture, we seek constant creative change. Life is viewed as a journey or adventure. The nature of the adventure, whether we are conscious of it or not, is to break every shred of attachment that keeps us earthbound while reaching for higher levels of maturity, higher states of being. There is an explosion of desire to live awake, creating freely while uncovering the character and nature of the soul and spirit within ourselves. There is a conscious desire on the part of many to live the life of *genuine wealth*—a life of loving, moral, selfless service that stems from a compassionate heart that embraces all things and beings.

Previous paradigms of how life is supposed to work are falling apart with uncommon speed. As trusted systems of life outside prove more and more untrustworthy, people find they have to let go of the beliefs that supported them. Sensitive people quickly discover that the best option for finding what is truly trustworthy is to turn inward to find their security and happiness. Walt Baptiste came to bring us the structure and techniques that show us exactly *how* to turn in. He taught us the value for following through with our commitments to live the life of the soul and grow spiritually. And he taught us not through books but by being a living example.

So, what is your life experience like when you live from your higher centers?

- You realize just how powerful you are at creating the life that brings you the most happiness. You truly are the creator of your life, and you have a choice about how you want to experience it.
- Because you are fully conscious of your talents and their service to life, every day is filled with meaningful purpose that brings a sense of general happiness.
- Now you understand that it's more important than ever for you to choose to create from the Soul Nature of yourself with its refinements and higher sensitivities to greater wisdom and intuitive knowing.

- Harmful ego-personality traits diminish substantially. Selfishness, false desires, control, manipulation, the habit of battling one side against another, loving with condition, a false sense of security: none of these influence your choices any longer.

Simply put, when you live from your higher centers, materiality doesn't have its grip on your life the same way it used to.

Can you imagine what it's like to experience the creating power of your genius minus your subconscious limitations?

Can you imagine the sweet, pleasant self-assurance you would have about yourself, knowing the *true* value of your genius and its value to the world around you?

Can you imagine who you will be and what your life will be like later in life because you've mastered why you are here?

Can you imagine sensing so clearly your connection with spirit, feeling Spirit's guidance every day so powerfully that you give up all fear of not being taken care of?

I once attended a yoga retreat orchestrated by Walt Baptiste's daughter, Sherri Baptiste. The title of her retreat was The Essential Baptiste Teachings. I thought "essential" was the perfect descriptive word for the guru's teachings. If you Google the word, you'll find two definitions. *Essential* can mean "extremely important," and it can mean "absolutely necessary."

If you are among those who are serious about adding the guru's teachings to your life because you want to live at higher levels of health, strength, intelligence, and beauty—in other words, the refinements of a higher humanity—you'll find the Baptiste Teachings extremely important. But if you are one of those souls who is very serious about spiritual growth, hungry for spiritual experiences, passionate about fulfilling your soul's purpose for this life cycle, or serious about raising your soul's evolutionary levels to the highest possible levels before death, then you, my welcome friend, will find the Walt Baptiste teachings to be *absolutely necessary!*

So, ask yourself—and be brutally honest when answering this vitally important question—do you carry a deep, passionate desire for spiritual experience, or do you carry a deep passionate desire to find, live, develop, refine, and master your soul's reason for this life? If the answer is a resounding *yes to* one of these questions, then congratulations. You are already engaged in the first essential principle.

Next, take a serious look at each of Walt Baptiste's disciplines—yoga, meditation, physical fitness, and a healthy diet. Start with the one you are the most drawn to, make it a comfortable habit, and then add another— until you are so engaged in all of them that they have become lifestyle habits rather than disciplines. Then, from your passion, respond to the inner urges that bubble to the surface, which are the result of the flow of energy moving through the form of the Baptiste teachings. This energy is asking you to explore your reason for being: your soul's deepest, yearning needs for expressing into Life.

But, let me add: approach each discipline with a serious intention for mastery. *Master* your yoga, *master* your meditation, *and master* your body's strength and health. And above all, once you begin, *never stop*! *Never give up for the rest of your life, right up to your very...last...breath!*

For more information you can contact me personally at www.souldiscoverySSL@gmail.com

More Time for Meditation
by Walt Baptiste

God-Realization is our primary quest and, our greatest need. For this is our cycle and season, our time to be KNOWERS.

A person (very fortunate) can have a Meditation "happening" by gift of Grace once in a lifetime, but to MASTER Meditation has much requirement.

To Master Meditation means SELF MASTERY. It is to Be Good and Do Good.

It is for the person who PRACTICES physical, mental and emotional purification.

It is for the devotee who masters the degrees of relaxation, inner relaxation, deep release and yet deeper inner surrender to encourage that the subtlest etheric element dominates.

It is for the person who spends much time in awakening the dynamic dormant Forces in the spinal Centers.

It is for the one who Practices constant repetition of Charged Words. It is for the one who understands the bringing the in-breath into out-breath and the out-breath into the in-breath.

It is for the person who becomes proof that one can have personal direct first hand "Experience" of the nature of Divine Mother and Spiritual Father far more real than imagination of blind faith or mere belief.

The "Soul" is liberated in the body because of much Inner-Experience. With all the above the mastery of CONCENTRATION is the KEY that opens the Inner Doors.

PRACTICE, PRACTICE, PRACTICE.

-Walt YogiRaja Baptiste

Made in the USA
Columbia, SC
28 May 2024

35964494R00088